# No Limit Parenting

## Do what you love and inspire your children!

Six Steps to an Extraordinary Life
for You and Your Family

*"It's all about your mindset!"*

**BALBOA.**
PRESS

A DIVISION OF HAY HOUSE

**Cover design and layout**
Nadia Azarova, www.azaart.com Kharkiv, Ukraine

**Editing**
Marije van de Bovenkamp, www.schrijfzin.com, Rotterdam, The Netherlands

**Illustrations**
Free vector art from www.vecteezy.com

**Translation**
Reggie Curiel, www.vertaalweb.com, Delft, The Netherlands

**Copy-editing**
Daniëlle Molenaar, www.virtual-efficiency.nl, The Netherlands

Balboa Press books may be ordered through booksellers or by contacting:

Balboa Press
A Division of Hay House
1663 Liberty Drive
Bloomington, IN 47403
www.balboapress.com.au
1 (877) 407-4847

Because of the dynamic nature of the Internet, any web addresses or
links contained in this book may have changed since publication and
may no longer be valid. The views expressed in this work are solely those
of the author and do not necessarily reflect the views of the publisher,
and the publisher hereby disclaims any responsibility for them.

The author of this book does not dispense medical advice or prescribe the use
of any technique as a form of treatment for physical, emotional, or medical
problems without the advice of a physician, either directly or indirectly. The
intent of the author is only to offer information of a general nature to help you
in your quest for emotional and spiritual well-being. In the event you use any
of the information in this book for yourself, which is your constitutional right,
the author and the publisher assume no responsibility for your actions.

Any people depicted in stock imagery provided by Thinkstock are models,
and such images are being used for illustrative purposes only.
Certain stock imagery © Thinkstock.

Print information available on the last page.

ISBN: 978-1-5043-0659-1 (sc)
ISBN: 978-1-5043-0660-7 (e)

Balboa Press rev. date: 04/21/2017

# Foreword

When we create a world where more people are doing what they love, a world where everyone is on purpose creating and contributing from a place of inspiration, this world truly can be a better place. It is my dream to create a world where doing what you love is the 'new normal'.

That's why I founded Authentic Education. Since 2009 my team and I have had the privilege of helping tens of thousands of people craft a life filled with purpose, passion, and love — regardless of where they have come from, where they are today, or where they are going.

It is my vision to live in a world in which each individual has complete alignment between their thoughts, feelings and actions. A world where shame, guilt, fear and judgment has been transformed into empowerment, appreciation and authenticity. As a father of a little girl myself, I want to do anything within my power to contribute to the realisation of such a world.

Children don't listen to what you say; they watch what you do. And therefore, it is incredibly important to be very conscious of our behaviour and the (sometimes unconscious) messages we send out to our children on a day-to-day basis.

As our educational system is often still telling the old story, that to become successful in life you need to do your homework, get good grades, go to University and look for that perfect and well-paying job, we as parents can make a difference. We can tell a new story, teach them differently and develop a positive growth mindset in ourselves and our children.

The best way to show our kids what else is possible is becoming the best version of ourselves and creating life on purpose for ourselves. Especially mothers are sometimes 'stuck' in the idea that they need to sacrifice themselves to be a good mum, but the exact opposite might be true. To be a good mum, you first need to take really good care of yourself.

The best way to teach our children that loving what you do is what we are meant to do in life and the most humbling way to serve others, is by giving them an inspiring example. To show them what self-love and self-compassion look like, and to provide them with the tools to make heart-centered choices in life.

That's why I am so appreciative about this book that you're about to read. Monique did a magnificent job, as she combines her in-depth knowledge as a child psychologist and life coach with her own life-experience as a woman and mum of four herself, in a clear and simple way. She generously shares her knowledge, techniques, tips and tools to apply them in your life and integrate them in the family as a whole.

Benjamin J Harvey
Founder of Authentic Education
www.authenticeducation.com.au

# Reactions / Testimonials

Monique takes you along on a very beautiful, inspirational and loving journey on how to approach parenthood differently. She shows you that if you think and live from a positive mindset you give yourself so much freedom. By looking yourself in the eye and daring to look at yourself in the mirror, you grant yourself the opportunity to arrange your own life and to find and be yourself. The most beautiful and unique aspect of this book is that it is an inspiration for the entire family! You can take your children along on this wonderful journey, learning and creating together.

*— Ruth Abigail Klein, life coach and*
*mother of four children, Thailand*

I became inspired and excited from the preface and the introduction on. Monique recognises today's challenges and writes in a realistic manner. This book will appeal to many parents.

*— Madeleine Thesseling, ortho-pedagogue and*
*family therapist, mother of 3 daughters, Australia*

I read the whole book in a single go! What a delightful book; clearly explained, easy to understand, and with useful assignments/ways of working that will make you think, and that are truly practical. Along the same lines as the philosophy of Wayne Dyer and Louise Hay, this book offers me excellent tools and input that contribute to my personal growth and development. It has made me evaluate my own qualities, my goals and the way I want to be in life in general. And of course about others (friendships) as well as in relation to the upbringing of my little boy. Great! Thank you for this input. I started working on a new vision board straight away! :-)

*— Heleen Meuleman, children's coach*
*and mother of a son, The Netherlands*

This book is a real gift for me as an independent entrepreneur and mother of four children in a combined family. Monique Daal has managed to write an inspirational, educational, honest and practical book. This lady has a vast amount of knowledge and life experience. In contrast to many other books that inspire me, the tips and assignments in this book, ensure that you can apply them directly to your family. In such a way that it brings about fundamental changes in the most positive sense. No Limit Parenting, in our house has not disappeared in a bookcase but lies prominently displayed on the kitchen table, to be frequently consulted. An insightful present for every parent who consciously wants to raise children and enjoy life.

*— Marije van de Bovenkamp, writing coach &*
*copywriter, mother of four children, The Netherlands*

First of all, I would like to thank Monique for this excellent book, which has obviously been written from her heart and her ever 'growing mindset'. It is nice to see that you always seem to open this book at the right moment. Therein lies its strength.

How brave are you when you open yourself up and take the reader along through your own story and life lessons? Monique shows us that you can free yourself from deeply anchored fears, shame and negativity and that you can grow in your own freedom, (com)passion and love, for yourself and for your family. Monique takes – aside from her family – everybody along, who is ready for growth, with the six 'C-words' in the back of their minds. With a mirror that can sometimes feel a bit uncomfortable, but the book emanates a very special kind of warmth, which cannot be missed!

*— Marjolein van Dongen - Lapré, remedial*
*educationalist and mother of one son, Curaçao*

# Dedication

I dedicate this book to my husband and my children because they challenge me every day to be the best version of myself.

They inspire me to live my life with passion, courage and dedication and to rise above mediocrity and negativity.

It is my intention to encourage others to do this very same thing.

*You can guide your children toward becoming compassionate, heart-centred adults who lead fulfilling, no limit lives.*

~ *Wayne Dyer*

## Gifts and bonuses

Buying this book will give you access to six extraordinary free gifts. Practical, creative and remarkable giveaways for you and your family, so that you can put what you have learned into practice immediately.

These free gifts are included throughout the book. At the end of each chapter, you can read where to find them and how to use them. I have created a special bonus website for this purpose.

It is my wish to inspire you with my story, and I hope that you will truly apply these lessons to your life. I invite you to take action with these extra free giveaways.

Free does not in any way imply that these gifts are not of any value. Quite the contrary!

Their value will become apparent immediately once you start putting them into practice.

www.nolimitparenting.com/bonuses

## Quick Response Code

To make it easier for you to find your way to the special bonus website, you can also use the QR-code; a barcode which can be read with your smartphone. The only thing you have to do is scan the code below with your smartphone. This way you can start working with your personal gifts and bonuses quickly.

Some smartphones come equipped with QR-code reading capability, but for other phones, it is necessary to download a QR-reader app first. To check whether your smartphone is equipped with a QR-reader, move your phone over the code below. Place your phone's camera in front of the QR-code. If your phone is fitted with the correct software, you will be automatically directed to the website to collect your gifts.

If your smartphone is not equipped with a QR-reader, then download one from the app store or play store if you have an Android smartphone.

If you do not have any desire to use QR, you can still have access to all bonuses by visiting:

www.nolimitparenting.com/bonuses

Should you have any trouble finding your unique gifts, please send an email to support@moniquedaal.com and together we will find a solution.

# Contents

# Preface

Amongst parents, there has never been a period of greater uncertainty on the subject of raising children and never before have so many mothers felt chronically tired, stressed out or worried. The reasons are not far-fetched: there is an ever growing number of professionals who cannot wait to tell you how you should raise your children.

Even the government will often scrutinise the way children are raised and direct the blame toward parents the minute some societal problem arises. Add to this a growing number of children who are finding it more and more difficult to adjust to school together with parents who judge other parents critically and hand out unsolicited and less than subtle advice on each other's child rearing practices.

On top of that, many women find themselves stuck in the middle of finding a perfect balance between raising their children, including all related commitments and concerns and their personal growth as human beings and as professionals. Mothers, after all, do have their ambitions and their dreams! But more often than not there seems to be very little time and space available to them during the period in their lives that coincide with childbirth and raising children.

Those who do stick out their necks or have the courage to want more out of life, typically receive very little support or encouragement from their environment and end up disillusioned and tired. When I started out with my company, my daughter was two years old, and people often gave me strange looks. Had I considered how hard it would be to start my own business? And what about the financial uncertainty?

The time set aside for raising and educating children does not seem to be viewed by many as the best time in your life to work on your personal development or your career, let alone start a company. For this reason, many mothers barely manage to display a fraction of their talents and their qualities. They manage to keep a low profile or put off their desires until some future moment. They are convinced that now is not the time for their ambitions.

Despite this, I have written a blog about the many parallels between raising children and starting and expanding a business. On many fronts, a similar set of skills is required, such as resourcefulness, patience, passion, perseverance and vision. Perhaps that is the reason why female entrepreneurs are often very successful.

I too was one of those mothers who kept thinking that her time would come and who also kept putting off her needs. I dared not to go all out for what I wanted; my business was doing okay, and I liked what I did, but still I did not show my full potential. In the meantime, I embarked on a journey to find more meaning and purpose and to find myself. I have learned a great deal during this time, and these are the lessons I wish to share with you.

Over the past 20 years, I have worked with many mothers, individually and in groups, as their coach and their trainer. Each and every one of these mothers wanted what was best for their child, but many of them felt apprehensive about the question of whether or not they were on the right track. I saw the concerns, the doubts, the frustrations and the fatigue. But I also saw their beautiful core, their unrelenting love for their children, their energy, their flexibility and their resilience. A lot of mothers are inclined to think: my time will come. But your time is now!

In this book, I want to inspire you in five concrete steps how to give your life a much-needed boost, to make the choices that are right for you to help you live a more tranquil life, with more love and passion.

That is to say in the midst of raising and caring for children, keeping yourself in shape, being a good partner and a loyal friend, driving the children to all kinds of activities, building a career, fixing school lunches, attending dinner parties with friends, that this all should be done with the kind of attention that makes you happy.

What I would love most is to see parents to be able to relax more and do more of what makes them truly happy. I believe this will make us better parents, more content and an inspiration to our children.

When you stop trying to do things based purely on willpower, or shaping your life according to the expectations of others, to start acting more out of love and trust, you will release a different kind of energy. A type of energy you probably were not even aware of and you will discover that you can arrange your life exactly the way you want to.

My wish is to share my story with you, and that my suggestions are meaningful to you and allow you to become the confident and sparkling mother you not only wish to become but also can become, whilst at the same time being able to become a resplendent figure in business and in your life!

Love,
Monique

# *Introduction*

The first time I encountered the term 'no-limit thinking' was through the books of Dr Wayne Dyer. A world famous inspirational speaker and bestselling author, who died in 2015 and who had a tremendous impact on the lives of millions of people.

In many of his books, the well-known self-help books for adults, as well as his lesser known, but equally inspiring children's books, he speaks of 'no-limit thinking' and 'no-limit people'.

His beautiful and positive message to the world is that everyone can make his or her dreams come true in this life. Or put otherwise; this is our only task here on earth.

He stimulates the reader to hold on to the limitless way of thinking we are born with, and to choose our path, rather than to conform to the expectations of others or of society. He also states that we can best achieve this when we live out our passion, and make ourselves subordinate to a greater whole.

Wayne Dyer has been a great source of inspiration in my personal and spiritual development. As has Louise Hay, author of the world-renowned book 'You can heal your life' and founder of Hay House, an outstanding publishing house specialising in books and products in the areas of positive psychology and 'self-empowerment'.

Both of them have made the universal laws of life easily accessible to a large audience and their books have been equally enlightening and helpful to me. During the last ten years, which have personally been rather tumultuous for me, I read everything on these subjects I was able to get my hands on And through trial and error, I experimented with their ideas and made them my own. These laws have significantly lightened my life and definitely made it more enjoyable.

Looking back on this eventful and instructive period, it struck me that I, a thirty-something, developmental psychology graduate had to search for books, videos, workshops and training sessions, to find answers to the questions that everyone, at one point or other in their lives, asks.

Why were these lessons not taught to me at school or university, especially as I was studying psychology? It is remarkable how much attention is paid to the gathering of knowledge and the ingraining of desired behavioural patterns and manners, and how little is dedicated to life skills that in the end will greatly determine our happiness.

In the meantime, I had become a mother of four beautiful children. In my experience there is very little information to be found in parenting books on matters such as handling stress or fear, about enjoying every moment, or how to manage grief and setbacks when raising children. Even though these subjects are addressed more often nowadays, it still does not outweigh the amount of help and information available on the themes of learning and behavioural problems at school.

Our modern society adds great value to the cognitive domain when it comes to the education and formation of our children. The world of thinking, of gathering knowledge, and gaining a diploma.

If we ask a random group of parents what they wish for their children, or what it is that they want to pass on to their children, you will invariably hear comments such as; I want my children to be happy; I want them to value and pursue their passions and ideals. I also want them to be able to handle themselves in whichever situation they may find themselves.

My background as a developmental psychologist began to clash more and more with the new ideas that I developed during my personal journey in search of more happiness and balance, and also in my role as a mother of four very self-willed children.

## *In search of a new paradigm*

During my studies, I specialised in children's development, from birth up to adulthood. How does the average child develop? How can I give early warning that a child is lagging behind in certain areas? How do I treat the child to get him or her to accept certain limitations or to latch on to the average developmental curve once again, as soon as possible?

Even though this model was applied to the physical as well as the social, emotional and cognitive development of children, it remained a medical biological or clinical approach as a whole which was primarily based on research among white middle-class families.

In the meantime, my personal ideas on raising children and their development started to shift. People like Louise Hay and Wayne Dyer have made me aware of the greatness of life and the power of our thoughts and convictions.

Finding your strength, getting out of the victim role and taking responsibility is an important common thread in their work. I discovered that we are capable of so much more than we often believe. We usually only use a small amount of our potential, and I think that this is a real shame. Why do we not dare to dream big and get more out of life? If we live to our full potential, it means that we are better equipped to help others be of use, and this will certainly contribute to making the world a better and more beautiful place.

I now believe that each and every human being can achieve great things. I believe that there is something here to learn for everyone, something to give and something to contribute. I no longer believe in shortcomings. Everyone has his place in this world.

It is our mission, especially when rearing and teaching our children, to grant them the opportunity to come in contact with their deepest desires, their talents and their resilience.

This insight has inspired me to develop the online No Limit Parenting programme and to write this book, which revolves around cultivating and allowing the correct and positive mindset to flourish. It is all about your mindset, which is what No Limit Parenting is all about.

As mentioned, I have four children of my own. My eldest is 17 years old now, and the youngest is nine. The great adventure of raising children can also be a huge challenge and is not always easy. My professional background in child development provided no advantage at all when it came to making the right decisions in regards to raising my own children, and the decisions seem endless: Mum, can I go and play outside? Mum, can I have a lolly? Mum, can I build a hut? Mum, can I join the gymnastics team? Time and time again those moments of decision. Is it safe? Is it educational? Do I have a clear view of all the consequences? Does my child have an overview of what could happen? Whether I say yes or no now, is that a good thing or just the opposite?

You need a guideline, a decision-making model, which you can use time and again to quickly reach the right decisions.

Looking back on it now I can clearly see my insecurity after my first baby was born. And even now I can often see myself faltering. The only difference now is that I have learned a few valuable lessons along the way.

- ✓ Make sure that you feel good about yourself and that you have your own space. This will allow you to relate to your children with more humour, patience and attention.

- ✓ There is no standard approach available when it comes to raising your children. They are all individuals and today's children wish to be seen and treated as such.

- ✓ Whatever you do or try to do: yelling, arguments, fights, and resistance, are all part of it but open communication and a positive approach will make sure that mutual relations are strengthened each and every time. In the end, this will lead to a firm foundation as a family.

- ✓ A system of punishment and reward will only help temporarily, but will not resolve the underlying patterns. I do not believe in punishment.

- ✓ Giving trust and responsibility is the key to more harmony.

## *So what is this No Limit Parenting?*

No Limit Parenting encourages parents to overcome their shortcomings and their own (often unconscious) limitations. That way parents can welcome their children to follow them and guide them to the complete fulfillment of their potential.

No Limit Parents actively stimulate their children to dare to push their boundaries. To not let them be influenced by the opinion of others, the expectations of society or their personal fears. They teach their children to listen to their bodies and their inner wisdom.

The intention of No Limit Parenting is to educate children at an early age to practice self-regulation, to be self-reliant, to have self-confidence and self-respect. To become children who can fend for themselves in today's world, even when mum and dad are not around to guide them.

## *No Limit Parenting creates No Limit People*

Through this way of thinking about parenting, I want to let our children know that everything in life is possible. And that happiness is in your head and your thoughts and convictions.

No Limit People are people with a large dose of self-respect, self-confidence and self-appreciation, regardless of the situation they are in. They feel at home in this world, and they realise that everything is connected. They enjoy going out to discover new things, and they possess a curious and open attitude. They see the wonder in the unexpected and the little things.

They experience anger or fear, but they do not let these emotions limit or engulf them entirely. They do not complain much, and they take life as it comes. They are not broody and have little space or tolerance for drama in their lives.

No Limit People experience a strong sense of purpose, and they have clear goals. They are willing to work hard and do not give up quickly when trying to achieve them.

They have an eye for detail, beauty and love in life, and they feel a shared responsibility for the whole. They feel a sense of societal involvement, and they are allergic to pigeonholing people on the basis of their religion, race or origin.

No Limit People know that happiness comes from within and they do not constantly compare themselves to others. They are aware of their uniqueness and their capabilities. They look after their bodies and minds and are hardly susceptible to depression or addictions. They do not wish to poison themselves.

They are creative, and they are excellent out-of-the-box thinkers. They accept the fact that because of this they tend to deviate from what society considers being the norm. No Limit People are inspirational people, and it is a great joy to be around them.

## No Limit Parenting is about you!

Every parent wishes their children to be happy, and No Limit Parenting aims to teach your child how to be just that. It starts by teaching parents how to be happy first. Children learn a great deal from what we tell them, but they learn mostly from who we are and the way we approach things.

That is why No Limit Parenting is firstly an invitation for you. I invite you to start working on yourself, to seek what it is that you want and how you can start enjoying life more. It is an invitation to boost your self-confidence as well as your confidence in life. This confidence is fundamental to be able to offer the right tools to your children.

# Prologue

Before you take that first step on your journey to leading this extraordinary life, I would like to share a couple of things with you. The information and insights which I am about to offer you constitutes my personal mix of knowledge and expertise as a psychologist, a coach and a trainer, in combination with my own experiences and information from a myriad of books, seminars, webinars and training sessions which I have attended in the field of personal development.

I am a very pragmatic person, and I want to be able to apply the knowledge and information which I gather on and offline, in my day to day life. I am the type of person that likes to try out things in real life and assess them, based on how it benefits my personal development. Does this bring me closer to the person that I really am and who I want to be? I am a hands-on person, always active and filled with ambition.

Much of what you will read in this book, has a spiritual base. I sometimes have a little difficulty with the term 'spirituality'. It seems to be the latest buzzword, and people use it in so many contexts. Also, I am, out of principle, not an advocate of labels or labelling.

I was raised in a Roman Catholic environment and even though I am no longer a practitioner, the seed of the idea that we are part of a much larger whole was most likely planted there. I do not feel that I am a religious person; I am, however, open to all religions. Is that spiritual?

If I can't sleep and I am tossing and turning in my bed, I have now learnt that yoga and meditation can restore my balance. That my head will find rest and that the adrenaline level in my body will go down. I enjoy reading anything I can get my hands on, about the universal laws, about self-empowerment, about the power of our thoughts and convictions, as well as about how we can feel better about ourselves and develop as human beings. Does that make me spiritual?

Spirituality for me is about walking the path on the road to pure freedom, fulfillment, and happiness. About limitless giving and receiving. To me, spirituality is walking your path in such a way that only befits you and you alone, and it is also about giving yourself permission to be totally you, in every situation. That you may have the courage to free yourself completely of all the conditioning that has been given to you during your life, and allow yourself to search for what is right for you. That you always keep searching, always guided by love, compassion, self-care and care for the world. That you connect with your true desires and give expression to them and share with the world. If this is the definition of spirituality, then yes, I am a spiritual being. And deep inside I believe that we all are. You too.

You also have a limitless supply of love and compassion within you, and you are also here to lead that extraordinary life. But 'the inner work must be done'; so get working on yourself! The only thing keeping you from living it to your full potential is you. This is a challenge for many of us. With my book, I want to help you take that challenge head on. To look at yourself in all truthfulness and to see what and how you can change to become more of who you are and who you want to be. To be a beautiful example for your children.

That can be an emotional rollercoaster. I know this from personal experience. By telling you this from the start, I want to prevent you from panicking, from thinking that your feelings are strange, and from letting these emotions stop you from continuing your journey. Know that this is part of it, that each and every one of us experiences these feelings. Know also that it will pass. That this awful feeling that creeps up on you when your old convictions are challenged will go away. Just like the clouds in the sky on a cloudy day, when the sky breaks open again, and suddenly the sun shines brightly once again.

Should you require help or support while reading this book, do check my websites at www.moniquedaal.com and www. nolimitparenting.com, or send me an email so that I can support you in many different ways during your process.

Because of my online programme, I know that this book, and what I share within it with you, can cause inner unrest, insecurity, and fear. Allow this to happen; you do not have to do this alone. When it happens, look at it as a present, because it means that you are ready for growth.

A beautiful visualisation someone gave to me during one of these moments is the following:

Look at yourself, with that fear in you, that restless and uncomfortable feeling. Feel it.

Ask yourself now: What is the worst that can happen to you?

See it before you. Watch this drama unfold in front of your eyes. And then see how you are handling it. Watch how you are solving it. Watch what you do and how you feel. Know that you can do this.

And when you start to calm down, ask yourself another question: What is the best that can happen to me now? What if everything goes well and what if I overcome this?

See it in front of you. Watch this incredible scenario as it unfolds in front of your eyes, and feel how that feels.

That feeling of joy, hope and trust.

Start reading this book with that feeling and I promise you that things will happen which will forever change your life.

# *Part 1*

## Have the Confidence to Love Yourself: Take Care of Yourself

*You've been criticising yourself for years, and it hasn't worked. Try approving of yourself and see what happens.*

*——Louise Hay*

# Cultivate Your Self-Esteem and That of Your Children

A positive self-image is essential for the development of children. It is the basis. The best way for you as a parent to pass this on is to work on your own self-esteem. This way, you give a positive shift to your own success and happiness. Developing a positive self-image is tightly interwoven with your outlook of the world. Genuinely loving and accepting yourself is neither frivolous nor selfish. It is the first step to an incredible and more fulfilling life.

Being kind to yourself is vital for your mental and physical well-being. Whether you call it self-love or self-care, it is critical for you to free up time for this process without feeling guilty for not being available for others or that you are acting irresponsibly or wasting your valuable time. It is just like the oxygen mask in the plane. Just before you take off, you learn that you must put on the mask before you help your child or someone else. Know that by taking good care of yourself, you will have more to offer the other person.

Not everyone is good at this. Women especially have the tendency to put themselves in second place. You take care of your partner, your children, your parents, your colleagues, and your customers, but in doing so, it is easy to forget about caring for yourself. Remember that you are important too!

Being kind to yourself has to do with taking good care of yourself and your body. It has to do with accepting yourself completely (including those aspects that you may either not be entirely happy with or may even be ashamed of). With getting to know what your needs are by forgiving yourself, not feeling guilty, and daring to say no sometimes.

Being kind to yourself also means loving yourself and feeling love for yourself. Loving yourself may sound selfish. "Isn't this selfish or arrogant?" you might ask yourself. The answer is no. Loving yourself is fundamental to leading a joyful and positive life. It is the foundation that will enable you to turn negative and obstructing barriers around. So today you are allowed to divert your undivided attention to the most important person in your life: *you.*

# Chapter 1: How Is Your Self-Image?

Self-image is about how you perceive yourself, about how you see yourself as a human being, and about what characteristics apply to you. It is also about what you are good at, how you get along with others, how you react to problems, how you feel about the way you look, how you learn, et cetera. Your self-image is important in regards to the way you think about yourself as a person. Someone who believes himself or herself to be a kind and worthy person will emanate this in a positive way.

A healthy self-image is when you know that you are worthy of just existing. You feel appreciated, loved, and respected. This feeling of self-worth has nothing to do with your financial situation, your position on the job market, other people's opinion of you, or your marital status.

You have a positive or healthy self-image when you not only know that you are good enough but also know that everybody else is good enough. Everyone is worthwhile, despite individual differences in intelligence, beauty, and wisdom. A positive or healthy self-image is unconditional, just like the love you feel when you first lay eyes on your newborn baby.

Continuously loving yourself unconditionally is the very first step to leading a happy, healthy, and fulfilling life. This is why I will deal with it extensively in this first chapter.

Consider the following statements. Do they sound familiar to you?

- ✓ You find it difficult to believe in yourself.

- ✓ You expect too much from other people, and this causes you to feel often disappointed.

- ✓ You do not think you are good enough.

- ✓ You are far too hard on yourself.

- ✓ You do not set time aside for yourself, only for others.

- ✓ You think that you cannot do something.

- ✓ You believe that others are better than you are.

- ✓ When you look in the mirror, you only see what you think is lacking and not what is good about yourself.

- ✓ You do not take enough care of yourself. (You have bad eating habits, you do not care about the way you look, etc.)

- ✓ You are afraid to speak your mind.

- ✓ You feel lonely often.

- ✓ You worry about what other people might think of you.

&#x2713;  You have the feeling that there is more to you than meets the eye, and it seems as if there is something that is causing you not to realise your full potential.

&#x2713;  You often find life to be unfair; others appear to be in a better way than you.

First, write down a few qualities and characteristics about yourself. Are you creative, careful, impatient, trustworthy, melancholic, energetic, cheerful, intelligent, or enterprising? Write down whatever comes to mind.

Check the list again to see whether you really feel that these characteristics define you or if these are qualities that have been attributed to you through stories or anecdotes from your youth. Through nicknames given by others or through experiences in life.

If several of these statements apply to you, then your self-image will definitely benefit from a boost. I will offer you various tips in this first chapter.

I obviously do not know how you have experienced this, but in many families, certain stories about children are exchanged during family gatherings. In this way, you learn a great deal about yourself through stories of others. These stories will shape your self-image!

This became painfully apparent to me during this past year and a half, during a difficult period that my youngest son was having at school as a seven-year-old. When I picked him up from school each day, his teacher would relay to me a ten-minute account of what he'd been up to. This might be walking through the classroom for no reason, refusing to complete an assignment, or looking through the windows and waving to his classmates after having been sent out of the classroom.

His behaviour went from bad to worse until I realised that he was standing next to me every day and heard his "story" repeatedly through the eyes and mouth of his teacher.

This "story" became his self-image, and it was becoming a self-fulfilling prophecy, a psychological phenomenon whereby a prediction directly or indirectly leads to the outcome of that prediction. If we keep reiterating that a child cannot behave, then the child will most likely start misbehaving more and more.

As of that day, I asked the school to send me all communications regarding his "problematic behaviour" via email and to only respond to positive news after school. At the same time, I would spend time with him exclusively during bedtime every evening. We would discuss his day, his behaviour, his feelings, his needs, and his wishes. I gratefully used the children's meditation books of Wayne Dyer. I wanted to offer my son some form of counterweight and make his crumbled self-image rock-solid once more.

## *Your Self-Image Is Not Static*

Thankfully, a self-image is not static. It changes over time. There are phases in your life where it is essential that your self-image grow alongside your social, emotional, and cognitive development. As a human being, you will always be learning and experiencing new things, and these will contribute to either a positive or a negative readjustment of your self-image. You also get to know yourself more and more over time. This can alter your self-image once again. Your self-image is not clay that you can shape, paint, and stick in the oven to bake and be done with it. A self-image develops differently in everybody.

During my upbringing, great significance was placed on doing well in school, on the need to choose a profession that paid well (because I had expensive taste!), on being polite and well mannered, on having respect for the elderly, and on listening to my parents. By themselves these were all ethical educational values, although they were externally focused. My self-image developed accordingly. I was mainly busy trying to satisfy the requirements that were, apparently, the measure of being a good daughter.

At university, I developed a great need to get to know myself. Who was I? What were my values? And what did I want to do with the rest of my life? In short, my inward journey had begun. I often felt lost in groups; I was insecure about the way I looked and about my capabilities. I could not handle criticism well, and I often felt an emptiness inside of me, which I could not pinpoint.

By deepening the power of my thoughts, I discovered that I could shape my self-image according to my personal aspirations, which I found to be challenging.

Think about it. The question is then no longer "What image do you have of yourself now?" but "What image do you have of your ideal self? Who do you wish to be?" You can shape your self-image depending on what you want it to be, and you do not have to let yourself be defined by what others have either thought or said of you in the past.

For example, I never considered myself to be an athletic kind of person. I was modest, always felt selfconscious, and thought of myself as being the social type. That was the image I had of myself, which had partly been created as a result of what others told me or impressed on me via their comments or their behaviour.

What if I decide that as of now, I am athletic, at ease in the spotlight, and comfortable to be alone? Many athletes or successful entrepreneurs use visualisation as an instrument to adjust the image they have of themselves. It seems that when you plan to lose weight and exercise more, it can be supportive to imagine how you would like to be. By visualising the body that you want to have, feeling how it is to move in that body and imagining yourself having fun in the gym, or taking a lovely walk outside.

For many of us, this is not an easy task. Images of ourselves have often been imprinted at an early age, and we have come to identify ourselves with these images We derive our identity from it, but you do not have to be who you think you are or who others say you are. Your self-image could start to work against you. It can sabotage you in your efforts to achieve that which you wish to achieve deep inside.

Know that you can be who you want to be. The only thing that you have to do is to change the thoughts about yourself. Later on in this chapter, I will discuss at length the question of how to achieve this. For now, it is sufficient to become aware of the images you have about yourself. Whether those are your own and whether you are satisfied with your self-image.

## *The internal dialogue*

We hold a daily conversation with ourselves. This conversation basically runs along the same lines every day. You can compare it with your favourite record or your favourite song. There comes a moment when you know the lyrics by heart. You automatically sing along, and you no longer reflect on the meaning of the words.

We may address ourselves lovingly and encouragingly, full of understanding and patience. It can however also be that we address ourselves in a reproachful, judgmental, angry and perhaps even in a despising manner full of rage.

Have you ever consciously listened to yourself? You should try it for one day, just for fun. When I first started doing this, it scared me. So many negative thoughts popped up in my head, while generally, I am a person with a very positive attitude. Experts estimate that as much as 72% of our thoughts are negative!

The way in which you talk to yourself will depend on the manner that you feel that you have to be or more often than not, the way that you think that others feel that you must be. Are you still with me? This image which you believe you must satisfy is dependent on your beliefs of what is good and what is bad. These convictions are so engrained in your mind that you hardly ever question them anymore.

Every day, with this internal dialogue, we deepen our daily stream of thoughts – the grooves of the record that play the song of our life. It often starts as soon as we wake up. What is your first thought? In her books, Louise Hay describes how she thanks her bed every day for the great sleep she has just enjoyed. Many wake up, however – after hitting the snooze button on the alarm, rather violently – with their first thought being: Oh no, already? I do not want to; I do not feel like it. Oh no, is it today that I have the meeting with that annoying customer? Or that deadline for the article I have been struggling with all week?

Not a great way to start the day. Let alone what many people think when they get up, walk to the bathroom and stare into the mirror!

The more we manage to shape our internal dialogue to a more positive and loving stream of words and thoughts, the better our lives will become. To achieve this, we must become aware of our thoughts first. That is the first step. Your self-image determines your self-esteem and your self-esteem greatly determines your self-confidence and your feelings of happiness

*Your life is a reflection of what you think you deserve*

Whatever it is that you wish to change or improve upon in your life, it always begins with the strengthening of your self-esteem. Most problems in life come into being as a result of our feeling of not being good enough. Strange but true.

---

*An example.* When you suddenly have to deal with a financial setback, it can happen that at one point you start believing that you are not worth feeling comfortable with money.

*Another example.* If you are not succesfull at having a loving relationship with somebody, it may be that you have a deep-rooted conviction that 'Nobody loves me'. Both convictions arise from a lack of self-love and self-esteem,

---

# I am not good enough

In her book "You can heal your life" Louise Hay describes how she helped people with all kinds of support requests. Whether they were of a financial nature, educational problems, relational problems or a lack of passion and creativity; the root of the problem was nearly always based in the underlying conviction of 'not being good enough', a lack of self-love.

We harbour all kinds of ideas about ourselves that limit us or keep us from changing our lives. These negative thoughts most often lead to inertia and 'non-action'. Do you really wish to change something in your life? Then the very first step is to become conscious of your thoughts and convictions, and allow yourself the space and willingness to change these.

# Chapter 2: Practical Ways to Cultivate Your Self-Worth

If your self-image has been challenged too much in your life and has received a few dents and scrapes, perhaps has even broken down over the course of time due to difficult circumstances, then you may not even know where to start. Perhaps now you realise that, after having read the previous pages, you are passing your negative self-image subconsciously and unwittingly on to your children, Maybe you feel bad about this or even guilty. You are probably wondering if the damage can be reversed or if you are still able to change.

Believe me, we are incredibly powerful creatures with an enormous zest for life as well as being very resilient. The power of the mindset can reverse everybody's ingrained pattern. You can create your future now through your thoughts and convictions.

And the good news is:

  ✓   As parents, we already know what unconditional love is; consider the image of that new-born baby on your belly;

  ✓   Children are born with a healthy self-image We were all once very satisfied with who we were.

This makes our task a lot easier. If we can succeed in feeling that unconditional love we have for our children, we can feel it for ourselves too. And if we can subsequently teach our children how to get in touch with that healthy self-image they had when they were babies, we will have won the world. How do we do that?

## *Do away with self-criticism*

First - silence your inner critic. We often operate on the basis of a personal image and believe we need to act and be a certain way. We condemn those parts of us that do not comply with this image and we try to put them away, suppress them or camouflage them. Every time one of these elements rears its ugly head, we condemn, criticise and reprimand ourselves. When we discover one of these condemned elements in another person, we also denounce and criticise this person for it.

We create unrealistic expectations in the process and as a consequence, we feel disillusioned, sad, angry, ashamed, guilty or unwilling if reality does not satisfy these expectations. We may even punish ourselves or others when we do not manage to meet the standards of our self-created image. We do not give ourselves and others permission to be who we are and to act spontaneously.

The effect feels restrictive and requires an unnecessary amount of energy. Living a life through these self-imposed images prevents us from noticing the good things in life and from fully enjoying ourselves and others. Do you wish to spend your entire life fighting against yourself or would you rather learn how to love yourself completely, the pleasant as well as the not so pleasant aspects of yourself? The choice is entirely yours.

# Accepting yourself entirely as you are

Each person is unique, and this is what makes every human being so special. Something you may see as a weak trait, or even as a bad thing, can turn out to be one of your greatest strengths in certain situations. The challenge is to achieve a clear image of yourself, the characteristics, character traits and personality quirks that you possess and to discover how you judge them, be it good or bad.

Then you can lovingly embrace all these components of yourself in the knowledge that the elements that you deem to be 'bad' can be of great use in certain situations. In the end, you can decide, in any situation, which elements to deploy and to what extent, to achieve that which you wish to achieve.

Accepting yourself as you are, the wanted as well as the unwanted elements of yourself, without adding the label 'good' or 'bad' is the only way to build a positive and realistic self-image.

# Investigate your own thoughts

An important step towards a more positive self-image is for you to become aware of the images and thoughts about yourself from your own internal dialogue. The next step is to further investigate these thoughts. A beautiful and valuable way to further examine your own beliefs is "The Work" by Byron Katie. She developed a way to trace and investigate the thoughts that cause all the suffering in the world. It is a way to find peace within yourself and to make peace with the world. Everyone with an open mind can do 'The Work'.

Byron Kathleen Reid became severely depressed when she was in her thirties. Her depression became more and more severe during a period of ten years. And Katie (as she is called) was barely able to leave her bedroom during that time. One morning, from her deepest despair she experienced a life changing awareness.

Katie learned that she suffered when she believed her thoughts and that she did not suffer when she did not believe her thoughts. The cause of her depression did not lie in the world around her but in what she believed about the world around her. In a flicker of insight, she saw that our attempt to find happiness worked in just the opposite way; instead of hopelessly trying to change the world to our thoughts about how it should be we can investigate these thoughts. By accepting reality as it is, we can experience unimaginable freedom and joy. The result was that a bedridden, suicidal woman was filled with love for everything that life had to offer. Her books are definitely a recommendation but for now, I will only touch upon her working methods.

The essence is that you distance yourself from your thoughts and that you investigate these objectively.

A thought will not harm us, unless we believe it. It is not our thoughts but the attachment we have to those thoughts that cause us suffering. Attachment to a thought means that we believe it to be true without having investigated it. A conviction is a belief that we have often adhered to for years. Katie encourages us to approach our thoughts with understanding. She says: "I do not let go of my thoughts, I meet them with understanding. Then they let me go."

On a daily basis we think all kinds of thoughts, about how something or someone should be, or about certain convictions that we have acquired. When such a thought causes you stress, ask yourself the following four questions.

Take the following thought for example: "I will never succeed at what I like to do most". And go through these four questions.

1. Is it true? (Yes or no. Go to question 3 if no)

Be still. If you really wish to know the truth, the honest yes or no will come from within you, as the answer to this question when you recreate the same situation in your mind. The answer to this question can only be yes or no. Investigate the 'but' and the 'because' should they surface and remain still until you are confident that the answer is yes or no.

2. Can I be absolutely sure that it is true? (yes or no)

Think about these questions: In that situation can I absolutely know that it is true? Can I ever know this for certain? We accept many thoughts as true, but we cannot deem them to be 100 % accurate. You cannot know whether you will never be successful because you have never tried 100% to be successful.

3. How do I react? What happens, when I believe that thought?

Be still, observe. For example: "I feel frustrated and nauseous". "I lose my calm". "I start to talk louder and faster". Finish the list while you observe the situation and allow the images of the past and the future to surface in your mind to show you how you would react when you believe that thought. Does that thought bring stress in your life? Which physical and emotional sensations come up when you believed that thought? See all the effects of believing that thought

4. Who would I be without this thought?

Strangely enough, we stick to certain thoughts because we get something from them. Even though, on a conscious level, we admit that the thought also gives us stress, we can be subconsciously attached to that thought. We use the thought to avoid having to do something about it or to avoid having to feel something. In that case, it can feel very scary having to let go of these thoughts, to imagine that this thought is no longer with you. You suddenly feel very 'naked' because this thought or conviction has been with you for so long. You might even have believed that this thought was part of your identity. Imagine yourself without this thought. How would your life be in an identical circumstance but without this thought? Take your time. See what reveals itself to you. What do you see now? See the difference.

The last step in this method is that of the reversal. Turn the statement around. Search for at least three specific and real examples of how each reversal is just as true or even more true than the original statement.

Search for opposites of the original statement or thoughts to accomplish the reversal. A statement can often be reversed to itself, to the other and to the opposite. This may sound complicated so I will explain further.

If the thought is about another person, change the name of the other to your own name or change he/she with me, and see what happens. For example: "He does not listen to me ...", becomes, "I do not listen to him", or, "He listens to me". Reversal is a powerful element of 'The Work'. As long as you believe that the cause of your problems is 'out there', as long as you think that something or someone else is responsible for your suffering, the situation is hopeless. It means that you are permanently stuck in the victim role. With the reversal, you take responsibility for the way you feel.

This can be confrontational, and you have to realise that it is not about blaming yourself or feeling guilty. It is about discovering the alternatives that can bring you peace,

A statement like, "I do not want to anymore ...", or, "I am never allowed ...", will be reversed to, "I am willing to ...", or, "I may ...".

This reversal is about embracing life just the way it is. Saying and meaning "I am willing to ..." creates openness, creativity and flexibility. Any resistance that you may have against the world will soften, and will allow you to open yourself to the conditions in your life, instead of using willpower or violence to ban it out of your life or keep it away from you.

Not every statement has three reversals, and some have even more than three. Certain reversals may seem like utter nonsense to you; do not force these. Nevertheless interacting actively with your own thoughts and convictions in this manner is a powerful and direct way to locate your own barriers, and organise your own happiness.

We often grow very weary of a particular thought. Thoughts that can make you feel angry, sad, furious, helpless, anxious, or depressed. It is sensible to question these?

✓  Can I be certain that this thought is 100% true?

✓  How do I feel about this thought?

✓  Who would I be without this thought?

✓  What helpful thought can I replace it with?

Most of the time we try to eliminate, fight against or remove thoughts with all our might. The effect is that the thoughts only gain more power. It is more useful to see the thought, to acknowledge it, put it in its place and replace it with a more helpful thought.

Even though you sometimes feel misunderstood by others and despite the fact that this makes you feel sad, you can choose to be open and willing to listen to your own heart and grant yourself the understanding you are so longing for. "The Work" by Byron Katie can help you with this.

## *Working with affirmations: brainwash yourself*

A different way to strengthen your self-image is by using affirmations. In my own life I have achieved many great results with this. It is important to use them in the right way and that you understand how this process works. My mentors in the field of affirmations are Louise Hay and in The Netherlands, Edith Hagenaar. Both of them have clearly described how to use affirmations as a powerful instrument to bend old obstructing convictions into a positive attitude. That is where the magic begins.

You have programmed your brain for the most part during your life. Your thoughts, your words are constantly programming your mind in a positive or negative manner depending on quality and content. It is the same with your self-confidence. Your self-confidence has usually been built up during your life. Even if you have a very low self-image at the moment, there is hope. Self-confidence is something you can work on.

If you have confidence in life, you are able to react in a more spontaneous manner, and you are not bothered about what other people think of you.

The extent of self-confidence is influenced by the way you think about yourself and what you tell yourself in your thoughts. Negative thoughts and convictions can hinder you. You will start believing your own negative thoughts, and this makes you insecure. Stop bringing yourself down all of the time. You are a precious and valuable person, so treat yourself as such.

Thinking is something that you do. You can influence it. Thinking, or at least, the way that you think, is a habit. And just like all other habits, you are the one who can control it. It is just like sports or dieting, you have to work at it.

By filling your head with positive thoughts, you can indeed produce a change in your life. If you repeat something often enough, you will start to believe in it. This also works in the negative (a callous parent constantly telling his child: "you are worthless", for example, will cause the child to carry this feeling into adulthood), but thankfully also in the positive.

If you emphasise enough positive aspects of yourself, your self-confidence will grow. Emphasise your successes. Literally. Give yourself a pat on the back.

Working with affirmations is nothing more than positive autosuggestion. You can influence your subconscious directly by using affirmations. Affirmations allow you to reprogramme yourself, as it were. Use positive words that affirm how you wish to feel.

## What is an affirmation?

An affirmation is actually every thought that you think and every sentence you speak. Without even being aware of it, you use affirmations throughout the day (I will never get this done!). Towards your children (You are really intolerable today!) and towards others (That is much too difficult for you). We use affirmations most of the time in a negative way. By consciously using them in a positive way and repeating them regularly you can change your thoughts about yourself and thus, your life as well.

If you wish to use affirmations to change your life, then, in the assertion, you must describe how you would want reality to be. By repeating this affirmation to yourself regularly, your brain will start to believe it, allowing you to experience this reality more and more.

If for example, you think that everybody is always nice to you, then the chances are that it really is true. The minute you tell yourself that, "This is one of those days where nothing goes right", and you believe that you will usually be right, everything will go wrong that day.

*An example:*

Suppose you wish to earn more money. You can turn that into an affirmation. You may believe that it is difficult to make money, simply because this has always been the case for you. Your own belief will be confirmed time and time again.

Write down the following affirmation for yourself: 'I can easily earn a lot of money'. Say it out loud and repeat it a few times. Write your affirmation in your diary or in another place where you can often read it. Repeat it regularly to yourself.

Keep repeating the affirmation until you start believing it. Somehow you know that it is nonsense and at the same time it feels like some sort of truth.

> By repeating it constantly you will reset your convictions
> concerning money and after a while you will notice that it
> will indeed become easier to earn money. Your belief will
> become stronger and your affirmation will have been a
> success; you are in a positive spiral. If you have achieved
> this, then it is time to start working on a new affirmation!

Affirmation reprogrammes the brain as it were causing you to experience the world around you in a different way.

Try it for a month. Voice your affirmation with feeling. You have to feel what the new situation will be like for you. The stranger or awkward the affirmation seems to you, the more inner work is required. Which resistances come up? Wat are your 'yes buts'? Define a positive reversal for every 'yes but'.

It is important when setting positive affirmations, to always do so in the present tense, like, 'I am' or 'I have'. Your subconscious is obedient. If you declare something in the future tense, it will always remain there, just out of reach, in the future

A good affirmation adheres to the following 'rules':

1. It must be positive: I am healthy. Wrong: I am not healthy.

2. It must be in the present tense: I am healthy. Wrong: I will be healthy once again.

3. It must be in the me-form: My body is healthy. Wrong: this body is healthy.

4. It must be active: I am healthy. Wrong: I want to be healthy.

5. Name what you wish to achieve and not what you want
   to avoid.

You will see that it does work and that it augments your self-confidence. Programme your brain with healthy and positive thoughts. Be the architect of your own thoughts. Whenever you have time use your powers of imagination to create a healthy and vital image of yourself on a daily basis. Working with affirmations is a playful and yet powerful way to steer your life in the direction that you want it to go.

## *Mirroring*

Louise Hay advises us to combine affirmations with what she refers to as, 'mirror work'. Mirrors reflect our feelings about ourselves back to us. The essence of mirror work is the theory that your life is like a mirror. The way in which you experience life is a reflection of how you experience yourself. How much self-confidence you have, how you look at yourself, how much value you attach to yourself … everything is mirrored in your life.

When I did the 'You can heal your life' exercise for the first time I became emotional. The exercise is: Look in the mirror and tell yourself, "I love myself, I accept myself completely". Look into your own eyes and become aware of your feelings. What do you feel? If you hesitate, feel resistance or feel very uncomfortable, ask yourself why. Which old conviction are you holding on to? The idea is not to reprimand yourself or to bring yourself down, just take a look at what is wrong and what thoughts arise.

In the beginning, it was very difficult for me. It felt strange to act lovingly toward myself. I was accustomed to being a 'strong girl' and to not complain or grumble. I was so used to directing my love and attention to others, to make others cheerful and happy, that I honestly teared up when I spoke these words to myself.

If you recognise this, then investigate where this feeling comes from. Face the reason why you have developed certain convictions about yourself, and subsequently thank them – because at the time they most likely had the job of protecting you or keeping you standing – and then lovingly release them. This is an important step that you have to take to actually discover the real power of affirmations.

When you start working with affirmations, and they seemingly do not appear to have any effect or nothing seems to be changing, acknowledge the fact that apparently something else has to happen first. You will need to face and let go of the convictions that no longer serve you. A beautiful affirmation to use in this phase is, "I am willing to change". This confirmation indicates that you acknowledge that it is still difficult for you to allow genuine self-love to enter your life, but you are opening yourself more to start receiving. Looking back at my own growth and learning the process, this mirror work, as well as working on my self-love, has been the most crucial phase to reversing my life.

Make time NOW, for yourself and for mirror work. The best way is to start off your day with it. When you make positive contact with yourself in the morning, you will have a great start of the day. Excellent phrases to begin with are: "I love myself", or, "I say YES to this day".

Once you have more practice, you can become more confident: "I will make this day the most beautiful day of my life. Life loves me. I will attract only positive people and events today. Everyone I meet will wish me well."

These kinds of phrases will give you recognition, and you will infuse the day with positive intent. It gives you a moment of awareness just before you rush into the day and go about your daily routine.

Just as with meditation, pay attention to your breathing; slow your breath and make it long. Look yourself in the eyes and say, "I love you". This can be quite confrontational at times, but with practice you will start to notice a shift in your mindset and your consciousness.

Mirror work is also excellent just before you have to go and do something you feel nervous about or if you have to accomplish something. You will make contact with your inner wisdom and open yourself up to positive energy. It will develop a basic feeling of security. A sense that you are always at exactly the right place in your life and at the right moment.

If you practice mirror work before you go to bed, you can turn it into a gratitude exercise. You can thank yourself for what you have achieved or done that day. "Thank you that you have ... today"

You can also thank the universe for the positive things that have crossed your path today. "What I am very thankful for today is ...".

The difference with affirmations is that you do this in front of the mirror, and you make contact with yourself by making eye-contact.

In my own quest for more happiness, satisfaction, rest and focus, I have experienced which techniques work and which do not. It requires practice, perseverance and patience to make these techniques your own on a level that will really work for you. Do not rush yourself and do not expect miracles, even though some techniques can lead to quick improvements in your life.

Aside from the tips and techniques that I have passed on to you, there are much more ways to generate more self-confidence and allow you to think more positively about yourself. Find what fits you, and experiment with everything that you encounter.

Radical self-acceptance and self-love is definitely the basis for a permanent change in your life. Whichever training techniques or exercises you may use, without truly loving yourself, none of these changes or new habits will endure.

Finally, I will list my top-10 of self-love techniques for you:

1.  Work with affirmations: Reprogram your inner dialogue

2.  Work with visualisations: See your dream life before you.

3.  Work with 'The Work': Take your confining convictions down

4.  Mirror work: Affirm and confirm yourself

5.  Tapping: Emotional freedom technique

6.  Keep a diary(writing): Increase your personal insight

7.  Meditate: Discover the wisdom in the silence within you

8.  Me-time: Be nice to yourself

9.  Let yourself be inspired by others: Surround yourself with love

10. Follow your heart: Build up your inner courage

# Chapter 3: Self-image in Parenting and Education

A baby never worries about the shape of his nose or the dimples in his baby bottom. Babies act the way they do, based on their primary needs. A baby will express himself freely when he is hungry, in pain or sad, without giving a second thought to what we may think of it.

But somewhere along the way a baby discovers that it can cause reactions with others, positive and adverse. People are social creatures, and they always want to belong to the group. They need affection and attention to grow.

This inclination for appreciation from others causes babies and subsequently, toddlers, pre-schoolers and adolescents, to attune their behaviour and their appearance to the reactions of others who are important to them.

Your self-image, the image you have of yourself, is therefore primarily challenged by your contacts with your environment. In the first place, mainly by the people that comprise the family you grow up with. Friends will play a role at a later stage, as will the teacher, the coach, teammates and the remedial teacher. By interacting with others, through the reactions of others and by comparing yourself with others, you are constantly adjusting your self-image.

What is important when discussing our self-image and that of our children is to realise that it is not so much your self-image that is developing over time (although it is always referred to as such in literature). It is the realisation that others or the environment attach an opinion or judgement to various aspects of your persona, and how you subsequently handle this is the deciding factor.

Because of this, raising children is not about building up their self-image, but about teaching them how to deal with the reactions of others, who can influence their self-image.

Because as much as you would like to protect your child from outside attacks – bullying, cynicism, negative remarks – every child has to deal with this at one point or another. And what we want to pass on to our children are the tools with which he or she can handle this.

## *The development of the self-image*

A baby isn't aware of his social existence, though in the second half of his first year he will start to recognise himself.

At around 20 months old children will start to recognise themselves in the mirror and photos, but a real self-image hasn't developed yet. When children are about two years old, they will look in the mirror and be able to recognise themselves and think, "that's me!" Toddlers start to realise more and more that they are a somebody.

A toddler will be able to describe himself: "I've got a ball, I can walk, I am colouring." But it is only when they start primary school that they start to see themselves in a more psychological sense. They might be able to describe themselves as shy or happy.

They slowly begin to develop a self-image. This development takes place throughout their youth, puberty and adolescence.

Teenagers can feel insecure, very quickly. Their self-esteem starts diminishing as early as the age of 12. It reaches its lowest level at approximately 15 years of age. After that it climbs rapidly again for most teenagers. The reason for the decline in self-esteem is because teens start focusing on others and not on their parents as they search of their 'ideal-me'. It becomes apparent to them that they have to prove themselves more to their peers rather than their parents. They have a very fluctuating self-image, because of all the changes they go through, through puberty. Even the slightest things can throw them off-balance.

The social world offers your child a view of other people's behaviour, he interacts with them, and he receives feedback about his own conduct. His behaviour only has meaning in a social context. His self-image is constantly developing based on the feedback he receives from other people. This happens in two ways:

- ✓ Via explicit feedback: individuals who tell him directly that he is doing something right, or perhaps just the opposite; and

- ✓ Via implicit feedback: from people's reactions he derives what they think of him

Your self-image is therefore not your own; you get it from the people around you. Your self-image is the image that others have of you and has given back to you, through their reactions and their conduct towards you.

You have probably been told from an early age that you are not good at something, giving you the choice of believing it and act accordingly. You no longer wish to do something, because 'you are bad at it anyway.'

To have a negative self-image (complete with the similar feelings of insecurity, guilt and a sense of inferiority) means that you do not value yourself highly. Sometimes you may even seem to have a plausible reason for this, based on mistakes you have made at some point in time. Or you may feel insecure because you have not studied. Perhaps you feel miserable about the way you look.

You may have not received enough acknowledgement, and you have started believing it to be legitimate. Not only do you perceive it as such, what's more, is that you will begin to act accordingly. You will tell yourself (subconsciously) that receiving little to no appreciation at all, is the way it should be. You may have become a perfectionist, constantly setting the bar too high for yourself, thereby disappointing yourself each and every time.

## *Why a positive self-image is important*

A child with a healthy self-confidence believes in himself and in his accomplishments, regardless of what others may think of him or her: I can, and I dare to that myself. Usually, a child with self-confidence also has a great sense of self-worth: It is good that I am. This is also referred to as self-esteem or a positive self-image.

Children with a healthy self-image can handle themselves well in all kinds of situations. They are more inclined to try out new things because they are not afraid to make mistakes. They know that this is part of the process and that it does not reflect poorly upon their self-esteem.

Also, the way you think about yourself influences your behaviour. A child that feels loved by his parents will be more inclined to do something for his parents in return, than a child that feels himself to be a nuisance to his parents.

For example, a child that helps to set the table will be appreciated by his parents and will feel good about himself doing it. A child that has not helped setting the table, because he thinks, "It does not matter, mum is mad at me anyway'" will feel this anger once again and be reinforced in his negative self-image. In this way, both the parent as well as the child end up in a vicious circle, which can result in a very undesirable situation that cannot be resolved easily.

Children with a positive self-image learn faster and better. They are not afraid to do new things. They are easier to get along with. They are better listeners and are more inclined to cooperate. And they are constantly being reinforced in their positive self-image, by the positive reactions that their behaviour brings about.

A child with a negative self-image is less likely to show positive behaviour, receives less positive feedback, is less liable to demonstrate new conduct, and therefore experiences fewer successful experiences, which in turn will only serve to reinforce his negative self-image. And so the self-fulfilling prophecy (as I described in the case of my son with 'behavioural problems) is established.

The chances for an optimal development and a sense of well-being is thus many times larger when a child has a positive self-image, i.e. has received sufficient tools to be able to handle negative feedback or setbacks.

## *Signals of a negative self-image*

How do you know if a child has a positive or a negative self-image? There is not a clear-cut answer to that question, unfortunately. Some children walk around with slouched shoulders, but many others camouflage their real feelings. They can act very tough and/or very popular, and in that manner incur the risk that their need stays hidden.

Children, as well as young adults, can feel very insecure at a particular stage of their lives. In most cases this seems to coincide with a major life event, for example, starting in a new class, starting or ending a relationship or if the situation at home is or has been turbulent for a while.

Physical changes, such as a growth spurt, or puberty, can also influence the self-image temporarily. The body feels very odd for a while, and it takes a while to get used to it. They may feel clumsy and insecure for a bit.

It is not always apparent when young people are struggling with a negative self-image. Young people do not wear their hearts on their sleeves during puberty. Add to that the fact that it is normal for young people to experience periods of doubt and insecurity in their search for their own identity. When these periods of uncertainty drag along for an extended period of time, it is important to be on the lookout for signals which may point to a negative self-image.

Insecurity among children is noticeable when they start to behave differently than their parents and teachers are used to. Children can become either extremely shy in certain situations, restless or exhibit hectic/funny (clownish) behaviour. Children can also 'let you know' via physical symptoms that all is not well. They can complain of a stomach ache or a headache, develop eczema or a different kind of rash, nausea or fatigue/not having any energy left.

With young people, it is often less noticeable on the outside. They often find themselves at odds with themselves, with others, with school, their identity and the meaning of life. They are bombarded by unpleasant thoughts. How can you filter those negative thoughts about yourself out? And how can you face life with more gusto and positive energy? Young people with a low self-esteem run the risk of ending up in a negative spiral.

Teenagers with a negative self-image will keep comparing themselves to others negatively. They often criticise themselves, think of themselves as being less attractive, or good or smart and will bestow praise on others (in their environment or in magazines).

A teenager with a negative self-image has trouble standing up for himself and experiences a sense of emptiness. This often manifests itself in some level of listlessness: Not starting anything, letting it pass when something unpleasant happens and refusing to intervene. Most of the time, this passivity is acknowledged first by parents.

Listlessness can also be accompanied with sombre feelings, depression and a sense of helplessness. The teenager has negative thoughts and loses hope that life will ever be better. He retreats within himself, meets with friends/girlfriends less frequently and is of course less cheerful and carefree.

Young people and children with low self-esteem, often react clumsily in conflict situations, be it either too angry or very fearful. These children run a bigger risk of becoming victims of bullies.

To help you determine if your child has low self-esteem, watch for the following signals:

- ✓ The child has very little or no self/confidence whatsoever.

- ✓ The child feels that he is not as good as others.

- ✓ The child avoids any kind of challenges because he or she is convinced that they will not succeed.

- ✓ If something does not work out, the child gets frustrated and gives up easily.

- ✓ The child feels that he is less intelligent than others.

- ✓ The child often does what other children want him to do and seldom follows his or her own plans.

- ✓ The child feels that he or she is not allowed to make any mistakes.

- ✓ The child, for some silly reason, believes that others think that he or she is dumb.

- ✓ The child is afraid to make mistakes.

- ✓ The child does not sufficiently stand up for him or herself.

- ✓ The child is disproportionately tense in the face of new or unexpected situations.

- ✓ The child hardly dares to voice and stand behind his or her opinion.

✓ The child has a fear of failure.

✓ The child does not or not sufficiently indicate his or her limits.

✓ The child gives off a nervous impression and is easily angry or sad.

✓ The child thinks themselves to be ugly.

✓ The child retreats into him or herself and is often by him or herself.

✓ The child does not feel comfortable in his or her body.

When you recognise similar signals in your child, it is crucial to devote time and attention to this.

## Cultivating on a 'growth mindset'

Carol Dweck, a researcher in psychology, makes a distinction between two mindsets. The 'fixed mindset' assumes that matters such as your intelligence and your self-esteem, are stable and fixed. People with a 'fixed mindset' believe that certain aspects of themselves are unchangeable. The logical conclusion is that the possibilities of everyone are limited, due to these set factors.

People with a 'growth mindset' see intelligence as muscle power. Something that can be developed. They have a self-image that can be developed and with that, they can open unprecedented possibilities.

The mindset that people have is the reason for the enormous differences in how they handle challenges, setbacks, and learning moments as well as how motivated they are and how motivated they remain.

Scientific research by Dweck and others has shown that children with a 'growth mindset' are more motivated to learn and achieve better results at school. This allows them to develop a more positive self-image and feeling happier. Thus achieving a positive spiral.

You as a parent, have a significant influence on the mindset that your children develop. Children with parents who are very controlling by, for example, taking many things out of their child's hands, develop a fixed mindset.

No matter how good your intention to intervene is, unrequested help is often interpreted by children as if they must be missing the ability or proficiency to do it themselves. When these parents – who themselves believe intelligence to be fixed, praise their children, they frequently judge the ability of the child: "You did not have any errors in your test? You are a smart girl!" That often has an impact on how the child considers a trait such as intelligence.

Parents who depart from the growth theory are more interested in the learning process, the attempt and the effort. By just giving hints when a child is stuck in a problem and allowing the child to figure it out by themselves, they stimulate the child's learning process, and they give off the signal that effort is important if you want to reach a goal. Children of parents who adhere to the growth theory generally adopt this learning method.

The relation between mindset and self-image was also demonstrated. Research showed that the mentality of children from 7th grade influenced their outlook on goals. For children with a fixed mindset the effort was the goal; a test was a moment to demonstrate how intelligent you are. Children with a growth mindset, on the other hand, had set learning as a goal; a test to them was a way to demonstrate how far they had come and how much they could still learn.

But there was more. When a test did not go as expected, children with a growth mindset were convinced that if they tried just a little harder, they would have achieved a higher score. They attributed their inferior results to manageable aspects. They adjusted their learning strategies: More effort, more time and more attention in class. Their results improved and so did their self-confidence and their motivation.

For children with a fixed mindset a problem arose at the moment of testing; because they see a test as a moment to determine how intelligent they are. Each negative result caused a dent in their self-confidence. They interpreted a lesser achievement as something that was beyond the limits of their proficiency (the stable, unmanageable aspects).

Many of these children reacted by lowering their effort: The harder they had to work for a test, the dumber they felt. On top of that, they chose learning strategies which were not helping them any further. They spent less time on their work, searched for ways to cheat or tried to find means to avoid the work entirely. Their results plummeted just as their motivation and their self-confidence did.

My children thought it especially interesting that children with a fixed mindset were inclined to camouflage their inferior achievements or even to lie about it.

The research data has taught us that the impact of positive thought and the development of a growth mindset cannot be underestimated and that it is of great importance that we as parents provide the right example for our children in this area. There are many different strategies and ways to achieve this.

A very simple mindset tip in this context is linguistic. Exchange the word 'but' in your language use for the word 'and' where possible, and notice what it does to you. It sets a different tone, and it adds a different feeling.

The word 'but' usually carries a judgement or comparison with it and this creates separation, while the word 'and' allows issues to coexist and works in an inclusive manner. It offers space and freedom. Try it out.

Examples: "I do not need you, but I enjoy being with you". "I do not need you, and I enjoy being with you".

"Yes, but ..." or "yes, and ...". Small difference in language usage, big difference in the experience. Use them consciously.

Another small word that can make a big difference is the word 'still'.

"I cannot multiply," sounds different than, "I still cannot multiply" or, "I am afraid in the dark," versus, "I am still afraid of the dark". By using the word 'still' more frequently you can positively stimulate your child's growth mindset.

## *Practical ways to stimulate a positive self-image in your children*

We frequently have all kinds of expectations of our children. Sometimes these have even been formed during pregnancy. And when your child does not meet these expectations we sometimes have difficulty accepting these parts of our children. In addition to this, children confront us with ourselves time and time again. The things about your child that irritates or aggravates you, are either personal traits that you would rather not have, or things that you are secretly jealous of.

Imagine that your child is very extrovert in his dealings with other people. Your child dominates the conversation and seems to be completely at ease. If this behaviour makes you feel uncomfortable, it might just be that you are also exuberant, and you may actually want to change this. You may, in the past, have received comments on it, and you are a bit ashamed of this behaviour.

Or perhaps just the opposite. You do not feel at ease in groups at all. You may even be extremely shy, and you prefer to make yourself invisible. At that moment your child is likely confronting you with a learning moment, something that you might want to develop more, but that you find very difficult.

In both cases, it can very well be that you will be taking out your own frustration or emotions about this issue on your child. Your feelings will in any case influence the way your child will react in those situations. You are actually burdening your child with your unresolved issues. A child will possibly not understand this. Why is mum angry? Why is she not kind to me at this moment? This causes doubt and insecurity to your child about who he or she is. And that could never have been your intention.

The funny thing is that when you start accepting yourself, and you develop more self-love, you become gentler towards your children. They also instantly have more room to be who they are. That means growth for the both of you!

Children primarily learn by imitating. They learn through what you tell them and from what you put into practice. You cannot stimulate your children to think and to live without boundaries if you do not show them this by example in your own life. You are their primary example.

First and foremost you must make sure that you strengthen your own self-image positively. Work on those issues that you feel uncertain about. Allow your children to see this or to participate. Children often enjoy it, and consider it natural to affirm together. Make it a habit of doing this together, in the morning or before going to bed. Look in the mirror together and voice positive affirmations.

As a parent, you play an important part in the development of your children's self-image. Your influence is the greatest when your child is still very young. As children grow older, the influence of others becomes greater.

How you react to your child's behaviour is therefore of the utmost importance for the way he sees himself. You give their behaviour meaning. You measure his conduct along the benchmark of your standards and values. What you say to your child and the way you treat him influences the way he looks at himself.

When your child is still very young, you are already planting seeds in his essence. It is essential that you are aware of what you are planting because the harvest corresponds to what you have sown. If you frequently tell a child: "You are acting silly again!" or "I should have known that you would fail!" the child will end up thinking negatively about himself.

If he hears these kinds of messages very often, they will be engrained in his brain. And once these tracks are formed a child will fall in these tracks for the rest of his life and will remain thinking negatively about himself. The opposite is also true. If you receive supportive messages at an early age, they will shape you in a positive way, for the rest of your life.

People are unique; there is only one of each one of us. Yet, children and young people often have the desire to resemble someone else. They feel that being themselves is not sufficient. They are unsure of themselves and believe that they are ugly or that they are not capable of doing anything. How can you help them to improve their self-esteem?

Adults have the tendency to react mostly on what goes wrong. The moment a child misbehaves, we deem it necessary to point this out. It must not happen again. We summon the child, ensure that we are satisfied that he can hear us, and we state that this particular negative behaviour must never be repeated again. The older they become, the longer these 'sermons' last.

Learn to emphasise the good as well; of course, you will mention it when a child is lying to you, for example, but also state how happy you are when he is telling you the truth. It is crucial to reinforce them positively at that moment.

## *Working with children on a positive mindset*

Just as we (adults) have to hear the same message over and over again in various ways before it truly penetrates every fibre of our body, the same applies to children.

By allowing children to get to know positive thinking, you strengthen the base for a healthy sense of self-worth. It is imperative to start with this at an early age. I will list a few ideas of things that you can do together with your children below.

## 1. Reading symbolic books and stories

The power of metaphors and stories is enormous. They sometimes illustrate much more clearly what something is about. This is certainly the case with children. Thankfully there are more and more books available that explain the power of positive thinking to children. Two examples which I have endlessly read to my children are from my greatest sources of inspiration: Louise Hay and Wayne Dyer. These books are definite recommendations. In "I think, I am", children learn the difference between negative thoughts and positive affirmations. Funny illustrations and simple texts show how you can convert unpleasant thoughts and words into pleasant and positive ones.

In "Unstoppable me", Wayne Dyer teaches children how they can hold on to the limitless way of thinking that they were born with, instead of trying to conform. This way they learn to enjoy life, to become true champions and to soar through life, on their way to their dreams.

I made up stories myself for my children. I told stories in which others faced similar challenges, and I voiced their feelings. And of course, I made sure that the others always discovered that they dared to do far more than they initially believed. Or that they incited different reactions when they approached a given situation differently. By speaking about others you can create more space for an open conversation.

## 2. Colouring colour pages

Colouring is relaxing and a great way to bond with your child. Colouring mandalas have a symbolic value, and you can ask your child to write positive texts on the mandalas, such as 'I can do it' or 'I am at peace and relaxed' or 'I am strong and can handle everything.'

### 3. Making affirmation cards

It is fun and inspiring to make affirmation cards together. Search for quotes, sayings and other inspirational texts together. Write your affirmations on cards. You can also laminate them. You can find appropriate images for them, or you can let your child make a beautiful drawing. Make or decorate a beautiful box to keep them in. Or put a card in your child's lunchbox every day or in your own wallet. Stick them to a mirror, your laptop or another place where your child can see them. Pick a card every night just before bedtime and talk to your child about it. Be creative, you can surely come up with more ways to incorporate affirmation cards in the lives of you and your child!

### 4. Making mood boards

By creating a mood board, you visualise your dreams, wishes or goals. It becomes more alive and by combining images with powerful statements, sayings or quotes, you call upon positive emotions that strengthen your positive vibe. Sit down with a pile of magazines or use pictures and words that you have downloaded from the internet to your own computer.

We make mood boards as a family every year at the end of the year, with goals and wishes for the New Year. Or to look forward to and work together towards the emigration to a new country, when we moved from the Netherlands to Curacao in 2009 and from Curacao to Sydney, Australia, in 2015.

To work on the self-esteem of your child, you can suggest that he or she place a picture of themselves in the centre of a large sheet of paper and surround it with his or her qualities, achievements and dreams. Because for children too: it's all about the mindset!

**Important lessons and insights from Part 1**

**For yourself**

- ✓ Really loving yourself is the key to a happy and fulfilling life.

- ✓ Your thoughts determine your reality and your life.

- ✓ Negative thoughts about yourself and about life are unknowingly passed on to your children.

- ✓ The first step is for you to become aware of your inner dialogue.

- ✓ Investigate your thoughts and choose to adopt more positive thoughts.

- ✓ Practice with positive affirmations. Mirror work or 'The Work' by Byron Katie, are wonderful methods for working at reinforcing your self-image and your self-esteem.

**In relation to your child(ren)**

- ✓ A positive self-image is a crucial element to your child's development.

- ✓ Children develop their self-image, based largely on the feedback they receive from others.

- ✓ A positive self-image reflects in all other areas of development of your child

- ✓ You can help your child by encouraging a 'growth mindset.'

✓ The way in which you communicate with your children has an enormous influence on their self-image.

✓ By loving yourself more and accepting yourself completely, just the way you are, you will automatically accept your child's behaviour and attitude in a more accepting manner.

✓ Practical things that you can do to help build a positive mindset in your child(ren) are: reading symbolic stories to them and making affirmation cards or mood boards

In this first part, we talked about self-image and self-esteem. Do you really want to work on these aspects and make them your daily top priority? Then the 'Daily Self Love Sheet' is a very effective tool. To gain access to this useful tool go to: www.nolimitparenting.com/bonuses or scan this QR-code.

# *Part 2*

## Find the CLARITY to make the right choices: Choose consciously

*Knowing right from wrong is really not very hard.*

*If you have to question whether you are doing the right thing, you probably are not.*

*– Mary-Frances Winters*

# Learn to Choose and Help Your Children Make the Right Choices

If you know which values are important to you, as a person and as a family, then you are providing yourself and your children with a strong inner compass. If you know what is crucial in the upbringing of your children, in your work and your life, then it becomes easier making choices. If your mission is clear, then your life is simpler, because you go back to the core.

When you want to change or improve certain aspects of your life, it is very powerful to make a deliberate choice or decision to do so. Nowadays we face so many different choices on a daily basis that it can be a little overwhelming at times. Even a simple visit to the supermarket can confront you with a myriad of options. How do you know if you are making the right choice?

Life just happened to me for a long time. Important decisions in my life were made for me. They either just happened, or others decided what was good for me and being the good girl I was I always did what was expected of me. Taking care of and feeling responsible for others became second nature to me.

Yet still, there was always something deep inside of me that said that all of this would pass and that there was a beautiful future for me in the offing. But as I got older I gradually came to realise that I had to take action myself to be able to find myself and to be able to appreciate myself. Deliberate choices needed to be made.

Looking back, there have been a few moments where I quite clearly chose for myself and my own values. Especially these tough times for me have strengthened me in my conviction, that everything is a matter of self-love and self-esteem:

✓ The moment that I decided to study psychology, instead of going to law school, which at the time, offered better career opportunities.

✓ The day that I decided to quit my job as a senior policy advisor at a large city council, and start my own business.

✓ When I chose to steer away from the 'why' question when my first son was stillborn. And instead decided to search for the meaning of his arrival into my life.

✓ When I chose to close my parent and child centre in Curacao, because it did not offer me the satisfaction that I had been searching for.

✓ The decision to never be ashamed again for who I am and to never again feel guilty about the choices I made or will make.

✓ The moment that I decided to direct my own life and to only do things that make me happy and give me a positive feeling in the future.

✓ The moment that I purposely chose to never worry about money again, or rather, the lack of it, and to trust myself that I will always be able to generate money for everything that I need

And in that context I made two important decisions. First, to emigrate to Australia (to push my boundaries once more and step out of my comfort zone) and secondly, my choice to develop an online programme as well as writing this book, to be able to inspire others to live their lives to the fullest and to offer the new generation a good base from which to do the same (living my mission).

And yes, every choice was scary, was new, felt like a risk. But for me, four insights help me to keep on making choices:

1.  Know your values and live by them.

2.  Expand your awareness, step out of your comfort zone, time and again.

3.  Know that you are loved and that everything you need will be available at the right time.

4.  Know that every choice is the correct one at that moment and that you can always make another choice if you need to.

When you dare to choose happiness, your life becomes a lot easier and more pleasant when you learn not to bother yourself so much with others. If you dare to follow your heart, you start to love yourself more and develop a sense of fundamental security. Sometimes life is not easy. You get sick, a lover leaves you, you fail an important exam, you lose your job, a good friend hurts you or you are wrongfully accused of something ... there are so many things that can throw us off-balance. These kinds of disappointments can interact in various ways.

You can become angry and frustrated because you feel life is unfair. You can shut yourself off, shut your feelings out, become cynical or depressed. It can paralyse you, you will not achieve anything anymore, it can make you manically depressed, or you may lose yourself in your work or in addiction.

You also have fighters: they keep going, and keep trying, purely on willpower. But sometimes they also develop tunnel vision. They stop seeing other alternatives and miss opportunities that arise, and they lack the love and the attention of others around them.

And so everyone develops their own strategy for dealing with adversity and negative experiences. These strategies often date back to childhood and are based on childish beliefs. That we do not deserve to be happy or that we are not good enough to lead a productive and fulfilling life

Setbacks become chronic in this manner. We stumble through the day, for years on end. And we tell ourselves that we are going to start the desired change tomorrow. We continue to suffer as a result of past experiences and issues from the past. We just settle and think this is what life is: unfair and difficult. "Life is a bitch."

So we suffer in silence, hoping that someday someone or something – a stroke of good luck – will take us out of our misery and offer us new opportunities, and if that does not happen then our childish beliefs are reaffirmed. "You see, it keeps eluding me, happiness is apparently not for me."

I was also stuck in this trap for a long time. Until I realised that I wanted to get more out of life than this standard 'okay' level. Comfortable, but somehow still leaking energy and passion. My ambition was larger than that.

So I made a choice and took a conscious decision. I want to lift my life to a higher level, I want to totally go for it. I want to experience more fun, and also more excitement, positive challenges and satisfaction. Because I think that this is the way life is meant to be, and I learned gradually that the more you take life into your own hands, the greater the experience of these positive emotions becomes. The whole point is to become more self-reliant.

With self-reliance, I mean that you are emotionally able to take care of yourself, take control of your own life, and not letting external factors throw you off-balance, and that you are actively working on a mindset that will guide you through difficult times. Even to the point that you will start to experience hard times as much less hard.

## Where do I start?

At this point you may be thinking: Okay, I want to lift my life to a higher level. But where do I start? What is the first step? What choices do I make and how do I know if I'm making the right choices? At this point, it is time to take a step back.

For a long time I was one of those busy mums who liked racing through the day in a flow of making sandwiches, handing out kisses, driving kids to and from school to sporting activities or to friends. Working, cleaning, picking up groceries, answering emails, checking Facebook and coordinating and consulting with my husband on trivial matters. With the feeling that I needed to fulfill all of these duties and obligations, because I was indispensable. And the things that really made me happy kept being pushed into the future and postponed.

You can only leave this treadmill by choosing to. The change only really comes by making clear and conscious choices. Life is a matter of making choices. But how do you do that? How do you make decisions that you will not regret? Choices that make you happy now and in future? Do you choose from the heart or with your head? Do you choose from your own heart or mainly through the opinion of others? Or perhaps you make choices intuitively? The art, primarily, is to consciously recognise which method of choice making you wish to apply at any given moment. Maybe you have a tendency to base your decisions on the opinion of others. In that case, it is crucial that you now choose from within yourself.

Which brings us back to the subject of this chapter: Making choices. To be able to get better at this, it is important that you know your own inner compass.

# Chapter 4: Searching for Your Inner Compass

It does not help to make better choices by thinking they are 'good' or 'bad' choices. It revolves around making a choice and making appropriate choices. A choice that really suits who you are, what your life looks like at this moment and what you find important. In different phases of your life, it may very well be that other choices are more appropriate. It is of particular importance that you never lose sight of what is truly important to you. What you really care about, are also called your values.

As a psychologist, I am always very interested in the why's of our behaviour and thoughts. What are the impulses that ensure that we get up every morning and do the things we do? And guess what? If this is not clear to ourselves and if we have no idea of why we do what we do, we do not develop our own identity and our life will lack a sense of direction. We just keep 'doing' what we are doing, and we have the feeling that life is passing us by. "Time flies," we say. Year after year, we continue to struggle with the same issues.

To find an answer as to who you really want to be, it is important to reflect on your values. What are the things that really matter the most in your life? If you have to choose between two options whereby one possibility encompasses your values and the other does not, then your values will help you make the more appropriate choice.

Of course, making a correct choice is often difficult because both (or more) possibilities may have different elements of your values within them. In that case, it is important that you stop consciously at every choice and decide which value you will choose. That way you can ensure that all of your values will be represented at different times. When you routinely ignore a value, you will notice it. You will become dissatisfied, you will feel that something is askew, you will lose a lot of energy, and you run the risk of suddenly feeling like you have to 'pull rank' after a while.

If you know your own truth, then you will have a guideline to live by. You have an anchor, and others will feel that. Children feel safe when they know that their parents are not 'winging it'.

A beautiful exercise to get closer to your values is the next one.

Answer the following two questions:

1. Name three things that define you (personal identity)

2. Name three things that personify you in your relationships with others (social identity)

To help you a little on your way I will give you an insight to my personal answers.

I love summing up my identity with the following three words: grateful, energetic and open-minded. I want to be aware of all the beautiful things in my life on a daily basis, and I have experienced that gratitude works like a magnet: it attracts even more beautiful things.

I want to be energetic. This is often difficult for me, and I make a conscious effort to stop saying that "I am tired". I want to savour life to the fullest and always remain curious as to what life holds in store for me.

Lastly, open-minded. I want to stay vigilant to avoid getting stuck in ideas and convictions that are no longer of any use to me or that impede me to see other people in all their splendour. That let me judge or that limit me. Benjamin Harvey said that he frequently and deliberately dwells on the question, "What I believe and what is not true." This will keep your mind flexible, and you will remain open to new perspectives.

The three key words of my social identity are: inspirational, genuinely interested and loving. I really want to inspire others. I want others to feel that I am genuinly interested in their lives and that our relationship is meaningful to me, as well as their difficulties and their triumphs. And finally, I want to be a loving person who is ready to help others or to encourage them.

So the questions I ask myself are: Am I still thankful, energetic and open-minded in regards to my relationships with others. Am I really inspiring, loving and genuinely involved?

Feel what it does to you and experience the love of self and the love of life when you live your own truth. We often live the life of another, and we desperately want to meet the standards set by society, parents, friends or family. But what do you stand for? What do you want your descendants to say about you when they are standing at your grave? What would you like them to say about their relationship with you? About your achievements, about your characteristics?

Keep these values in mind when designing your life, when making the choices you have made each and every day. This is your life and no one else's. Use it to promote your values here on this earth. Do not be afraid to show the world what deeply drives you. It is not what you do that matters, but why you do what you do.

Of course, this is scary thing to do. It is not surprising that when the time comes that you actually have to make a choice, you will tend to back down. But the sharper your own inner compass is, the easier it is to make choices in life. The more aware you are of yourself, the more likely it is that you can effect changes in a positive way, in your behaviour and attitude.

Choosing your attitude is something you can consciously do each and every day and at any moment. Thus you can choose to be proactive at any time of the day and to choose your attitude towards events that are happening around you. If you focus too much on the things that you have no control over, and you feel negative emotions (e.g. because you are angry, tense or restless), then you may feel deflated after a while.

The special, and perhaps surprising aspect is that we can influence matters more than we often believe. In the book "The art of being brilliant" Cope & Whittaker write about the 90/10 principle:

- ✓ 10% of your feeling of happiness is determined by what happens to you, which can be classified under the heading of 'Shit happens.'

- ✓ 90% is determined by how you respond to that 10%! This is the area where you have the choice to adopt a positive attitude and to choose a response to what is happening around you.

To give you an example: You have no influence on the weather. Even so, many people step out of bed in the morning feeling less than happy when the weather is bad, and of course, this affects your behaviour. Perhaps you walk around the house in a bad mood, resisting the idea that you still have to go outside. It can even influence your entire day, thereby causing your day to become less than pleasant. It also works the other way around. You wake up with your favourite song on the radio, you're singing, and you feel great. The day begins just that little bit better, and even your partner and your children seem to be a lot more fun at the breakfast table.

Be aware that during the entire day there are triggers that can affect your mood and your positive mindset. But please realise above all that in most cases YOU yourself trigger your feelings, of your behaviour and of their effect on others. At any time you can consciously choose to let the outcome be positive.

Stephen M. R. Covey, author of the bestseller "The Seven Habits of Highly Effective People", states that people only handle change well if they possess an unchanging image of themselves. This helps with writing a personal mission statement or personal statute. Your personal statute reflects your values and beliefs. It becomes a measure for everything that you have to deal with on a daily basis. Writing a personal mission statement according to the guidelines of Covey, is a relatively extensive process, and it requires self-examination to be able to go really deep into it.

This may be taking it one step too far, but hopefully the concept Covey provides excites and inspires you to think about your values and to better focus on what YOU really feel is IMPORTANT in life. What it is you want to stand for. A personal statute like this can be seen as a philosophy, a creed, or a manifesto. It is intended to show what you want to be (your personality) and what you want to do (your contributions and achievements) and it reflects the corresponding values and principles. You might consider a personal statute as your very own law to live by. We can allow ourselves to be guided by it during major, as well as everyday decisions, even when strong emotions come into play.

Such an inner or moral compass gives you an anchor, especially when shaping your life and making all the necessary choices that come with it, but some people still find making choices difficult. Choices can sometimes have enormous consequences. But it often means that people who find choosing difficult are afraid of making wrong choices, or simply afraid to make mistakes. In that case, we are back to Part 1: Work on your confidence and your self-esteem!

Make choices that support you. When in doubt, ask yourself, "Is this choice right for me?" "Is this the right decision for me?" If you do not feel confident, then postpone making the decision for a while. But learn to listen to that inner wisdom that tells you which choice is the best for you.

## *Conflicting values*

Everyone has multiple values. Sometimes certain values seem to contradict one another. These are called conflicting values. Conflicting values can make decision making difficult and is the most common reason why we delay in making them. When you push certain tasks, decisions and goals ahead of you time and again, then you are most likely dealing with conflicting values. Specifically, this means that you may think something else is more important. Which means that there is a particular hierarchy in your value system.

Imagine that for months now you want to clean out your cupboards, but you never seem to have the time. Or you have been wanting to follow a particular diet for years, but you cannot seem to find the right moment to start. Perhaps you want to start your own business, but somehow cannot seem to get it up and running. All of these are examples of procrastination. You have made a decision, but you cannot seem to actually turn that decision into an action.

Apparently there are other things that are more important to you. You give other things more value. Or at some point in your life, you have come to the conclusion that some values are incompatible.

How do you find out which values are really as important as you think they are? Answer the following question: If you suddenly had an hour of free time available, what would you do? The answer that comes to mind first is something that is strongly linked to your personality and gives you a high degree of fulfilment. This says something about what values are important to you. Take a look at the table below.

| Activity | Underlying value |
|---|---|
| Family visit | Belong to something/being a part of a greater whole |
| Getting a massage | Attention/relaxation/self-care |
| Working overtime | Money/control/status/security |
| Studying | Growth/progress/knowledge |
| Appointments with friends | Confirmation/friendship/sense of belonging somewhere |

## Putting an end to procrastination behaviour

Starting with new behaviour requires activating new values, but these new values sometimes seem to conflict with old values that you also find valuable. This indicates an internal conflict and prevents you from starting new behaviour or breaking patterns. Making a conscious choice is the most important step, but you will also have to take action to realise that which you wish to accomplish.

Imagine that you are an entrepreneur and you wish to grow your business (new value), but you are not fully investing your time in your business, because you also want to spend more time with your family (old value). Your family is higher up on your value system. Because of this, you will tend to invest less time in your business to take the necessary steps for more growth.

Perhaps you wish to start eating healthier (new value), but you frequently find yourself craving delicious food (old value). Maybe you want to go to the gym more frequently (new value), but you never have time because you have to work a lot of hours to pay your bills (old value).

The way to effectively resolve these internal conflicts is to connect these two opposing values together in your brain. In such a way that it becomes one and the same goal in your mind.

What helps is to ask yourself how achieving the new value can help you get more or less of the old value.

Examples:

- ✓ How can growing my business help me to spend more time with my family?

- ✓ How can going to the gym help me pay off my debts?

- ✓ How can eating healthier help me feel less hungry?

- ✓ How can cleaning out the kitchen cupboards help me create more spare time?

Subsequently think of as many possible answers to the question. As many as possible. This will add a new connection in your brain between the one and the other activity/value. The more answers you consider, the stronger this new connection becomes. The result in your brain is then:

- ✓ Growing my company = spending more time with my family

- ✓ Going to the gym = working on my debts

- ✓ Eating healthier = less craving for junk food

- ✓ Cleaning up your cupboards = creating more free time in my life

When you reprogram your brain this way, you will see that it will become much easier for you to actually get into action mode and making your resolutions a reality.

## *The power of choice*

To quote Shakespeare: "The fault, dear Brutus, is not in our stars, but in ourselves." We have created our current circumstances through the choices we have previously made. But don't forget: Not only do you have the possibility, but you also have the responsibility to make better choices. Living your life to its full potential does not require you to always worry about things or needing different answers to reach better conclusions.

The only thing you need is truth. Your truth. Do not allow errors in your judgement steer you in the wrong direction every day. Go back to base. The basic choices that account for the greatest difference in how you wish to lead your life. Choose the things that bring life, pleasure and happiness in your daily existence. And if you are not satisfied with the way your life is at the moment, do something about it! You have the ability to turn your entire life around in every aspect of your existence. It all starts with the power of choice.

## *Choosing requires guts*

Maybe you do not have the courage, but there is one thing that you must realise: Not choosing is also a choice, and possibly a very negative one. He who does not dare or cannot choose can become overwhelmed with a feeling of uselessness. Secretly you know that you did not do what you would have liked to do, and that can start to haunt you.

## *Choosing is risky*

You know what you have at this moment, and you do not know what the outcome will be after you have made a choice. But still, deep in your heart, you know that you want something different in life. And what is life after all, where you have never done what you actually wanted to do, just because you never had the courage to choose? Would that not be an intense disappointment?

## *Choosing is scary*

It feels so final, and you might be afraid of the consequences. Perhaps even of what others may think about you. Many of these thoughts are a form of resistance and fear. The best way to deal with them is to accept that you find it scary and are still willing to follow your choice through.

One consolation: A decision is never 100% final. Of course you can make a wrong decision. You can lose a great deal, correct. But you never toss out all of the experiences that you have accumulated during your life. You can always choose again. Maybe this time for something entirely different or perhaps turn back to the well-beaten path. Granted, that may feel like losing face. On the other hand: There is nothing wrong with a roundabout, a gamble or a detour is there? There will always be another opportunity to make new choices.

# Chapter 5: How Do I Teach my Children to Make the Right Choices?

Children also have to make decisions, more and more it seems, and sometimes at an early age! That is why it is also important for them to learn how to make conscious decisions that are also made from their heart and soul as well. The plethora of options in our modern society can overwhelm children and young adults and make them feel insecure. The necessity to teach children how to choose is, therefore, great.

Teach children the following:

- ✓ To learn to choose means having the courage to sometimes say no.

- ✓ You must face the reality that your choices may set you apart from the rest.

- ✓ Choosing also means that sometimes you do not choose other things.

✓   Choosing means standing up for who you really are.

✓   Choosing is taking a stand and becoming visible.

✓   Choosing is above all, daring and doing!

In our home, choices are often on the agenda. Especially making decisions about how you are going to approach certain situations or events. You can be put off by the bad things that happen to you, but you can also choose not to be put off by them.

Children will not appreciate the importance of making choices immediately, because it deprives them of the opportunity to blame others for their own problems. It sometimes tends to sound a bit like everything is your fault, but it is not about blame. It is about knowing that you always have the strength and the power to choose. And that your choices will affect how your life unfolds. The sooner we can make children aware of this, the more resilient we will make them.

## Everything is a choice

The most valuable lesson we can give our children is to teach them that essentially everything in life is a choice. In this way, we acknowledge that they have free will and that this is their birthright. And their free will allows them to choose what kind of life they want to lead. They can always choose how they wish to deal with life. This also requires you as a parent to take responsibility for your own life and your own feelings.

An example, if you're upset by the way a store clerk has spoken to you, and you are still ranting about it once you are home, you show your children that the clerk has a very large impact on you and your home life. So you need to practice how to set a different example to your children. You have control over what you think and the way you feel about this store clerk who you do not even know. Let your children see this by saying: "That lady in the store was very rude to me, but I am not going to allow her to ruin the rest of my day. I am not going to give it anymore attention."

Children, often unconsciously, inherit the tactics of "blaming" in dealing with unpleasant emotions. By inventing excuses for your children when something unpleasant happens, or by placing attention on the matter of guilt, when they break or misplace something. And also by punishing children when they tell the truth, they quickly learn that they're often better off laying the 'blame' elsewhere.

Our role as parents is to teach our children not to be dependent on the opinion or approval of others but to teach them to focus on themselves. So when your child comes crying to you about something a friend has said, you can say: "I understand that you are hurt by what your friend told you, but don't you think that you are making his opinion of you, more important than your own opinion of yourself?"

It is important that you and your child understand that it is not the friend who has upset your child. You do not have to give a big sermon but let your child know that he his focus should remain on himself. This way you keep control of your thoughts, your feelings and your life.

This realisation is of the utmost importance for building self-confidence and self-awareness. In our society, children and adults are encouraged to be sensitive to outside control. Many of us have become entirely dependent on gathering bonuses, gaining more power or a higher position and affirmation from others. Let us help our children find their inner motivation to make their own conscious choices.

Children do not need approval from others to feel positive about themselves. We as parents,also do not require that permission from anyone. So set a good example for your children. Make the right choices for yourself, you do not need anyone's approval! You and only you know what is good for you, and the same thing also applies to your child.

A child is the only one experiencing his or her inner world. Teach children that they can and must make their own choices, what it is that he or she wants to experience. Teach them to navigate using their own inner compass instead of looking for confirmation in the outside world.

Sometimes it's difficult because we as parents continuously feel that the world around us is evaluating our educational capacity. As a mother of four children, three of whom are very enterprising and adventurous boys and a very articulate and confident lady, I rarely arrive anywhere, unnoticed. Once we arrive at our point of destination, my children are usually busy talking or immediately inquisitive about their new environment. All eyes are often aimed directly at us. And I've often caught myself, frantically trying to keep the kids in line. Instead of encouraging them to be themselves. I am overly conscious of behaviour that the outside world expects from us, and I look for approval. It will not come as a surprise to you that the children have a very keen sense of my nervousness in such situations, and are even busier and more restless than usual, which usually means that I achieve exactly the opposite of what I want. True freedom lies actually letting go of the need for the opinion or approval of others. And to truly stand for who you are or what you believe in.

# 8 ways to help your children develop their inner compass

1.  Teach your child at an early age that there are actually no excuses and always focus on the inner world of your child instead of the outside world. Do not say: "You cannot help it, you have had an awful teacher this year", but do say: "You will always encounter people that do not understand you or do not agree with you, how do you think you can deal with that?"

2.  Stop asking whose fault or mistake something was and help your child(ren) to look for solutions. So if your daughter shows you a broken doll and tells you that one of her brothers has broken it, do not try to figure out which brother it was. Engage in conversation with the children and brainstorm to reach an agreement on how to avoid these situations in future.

3.  Allow children to resolve their own issues as much as possible, and do not let your precious time be used, over and over again, by acting as a police officer. Do not give in to attempts to make you choose sides when your children fight amongst themselves.

4.  Teach your children that truth will be rewarded and that 'telling' and 'blaming someone else' will meet with your disapproval.

5.  Set a good example. From now on, do not blame your husband for your bad mood, do not blame your parents for your emotional problems, and do not blame McDonalds for your weight issues. Live for your children, how and what it is to take responsibility for your own happiness!

6.  Do not compare your children with each other and do not refer to them with remarks such as, "You are just like your father", "That stubbornness comes from your grandmother" or "Mum was also not very good at maths". Children take these kind of statements as truth and will start to believe them. These statements will limit the child in the possibility of approaching everything with an open mind, and they take away the child's belief in his or her own capabilities. They will then develop a 'fixed' instead of a 'growth' mindset.

7.  Shift the attention from 'being right' to 'having creative ideas' or 'simply not knowing'. It is not always about knowing the correct answer, it's about insightful thinking and not being afraid to give the wrong answer.

8.  Stimulate your child to do what he enjoys doing and to develop his or her talents, especially when it may be different to what other children are doing. Cherish your child's stubbornness.

## Important lessons and insights from Part 2

### For yourself

- ✓ To change things in your life, it is necessary for you to make powerful and conscious changes.

- ✓ You can consciously choose happiness and positivity.

- ✓ Knowing and living according to your own values gives you relaxation, control and peace in your life.

- ✓ The stronger your inner compass, the less chance of becoming unbalanced by the opinions and expectations of others.

- ✓ Procrastination is often the result of conflicting values; the trick in these cases is to 'link' the seemingly opposed values to each other.

- ✓ Choosing can be frightening, but you can always adjust your choice.

### In relation to your child(ren)

- ✓ You can help your children make choices by making them resilient and self-aware.

- ✓ Start discussions using real-life situations on how to deal with all manner of choices in daily life.

- ✓ Give more attention and energy to discovering and managing their inner world (emotional intelligence) rather than complying with the demands and expectations of the outside world.

✓   Stimulate their uniqueness, do not compare them with others, emphasise the development of creative ideas, instead of 'being right.'

✓   Acknowledge the way your child makes choices and make him or her aware of this.

In this second part, you have read about making choices and about the power of a conscious decision. A very useful tool, in this case, is the 'Making Choices Cheat-sheet'; four different strategies that will help you become better at making powerful choices that are right for you! To gain access to this powerful gift, go to: www.nolimitparenting. com/bonuses or scan this QR-code

# Part 3

## Focus your CONCENTRATION to help you deal with overwhelming situations/emotions: Be mindful

*The best way to capture moments is to pay attention. This is how we cultivate mindfulness.*

*It means being awake. It means knowing what you are doing.*

*– Jon Kabat-Zin*

# Be Mindful and Teach Your Children to Enjoy the Moment

Mindfulness teaches you to be less judgemental and to be more focused in the 'here and now' in day to day life. This leaves you more restful and focused and gives you space to enjoy your beautiful life and to simply be happy. Happy people are a magnet for more happiness! Which is exactly what we wish for our children, isn't it?

There are so many demands on us as parents in our current society. Our busy family life, work schedule and other activities regularly contribute to a lot of stress. True, some parents thrive on stress and lead rich and fulfilling lives, but many find it difficult to find the right balance. Combining various roles in one day requires a considerable amount of organisational skills and versatility on your part, which can lead to exhaustion, unrest, or developing feelings of anxiety or depression.

Children also have to digest considerable amounts of information on a daily basis. The arrival of social media also means that they are nearly continuously exposed to new images and information. Some children have such a busy daily schedule that they barely have time left to just be themselves and to learn who they are and to explore the world around them.

Modern parents have become really adept at multitasking and so have I! However this is often at the expense of being able to give yourself and your child your devoted attention. Multitasking is a cherished skill, especially for mothers. Because the more things they can do at the same time, the more quickly they are finished. The problem is though, that you will want to do more and more because of this, and you end up having even less time left. You will end up being more rushed, and you will be inclined to want to do even more. It does not give you a tranquil feeling.

When my children were small, I continuously felt badgered. As if there was still something that I had to do or that I had forgotten. I could hardly relax, let alone sit still. I spoke very fast, and my voice was mostly high pitched. If I surrendered myself to 'doing nothing' for a while, I noticed that I would fall back in some a kind of lethargic situation. At that moment I could not get anything done anymore, and it proved to be very difficult to get back into action mode. This is why I preferred to keep the motor running, and yes I was indeed extremely productive in those days. Or was I? Now that I look back on this period or at photographs from that period, I feel amazed. Was that us? Look how cute the children are? See how young I was! To the outside world, I was successful, but the days seemed to slip away at times, and I had the feeling that I was unable to fully enjoy the moment.

We love to tell each other how busy we are as often as possible. Life can be especially gruelling when our children are small. We believe that this is the way it should be, that mothers of young children are chronically tired. I now know that things can be different and that you often achieve more when you do it with your complete attention to being in the moment.

Mindfulness is living in the moment and doing things one at a time. Doing one thing and not thinking about the other. So do not think about preparing lunch, warming the baby bottle and checking your mail at the same time as you are changing a nappy. Changing a nappy is changing a nappy. After that, preparing lunch. Then warming up the baby bottle. Followed by answering your email. There is a difference between having a lot to do and thinking about having to do a lot. The first is simply a succession of activities, the latter is stressing about something that is going to happen later on, as well as causing the quality of the moment to decrease. See your life as a series of now's and execute every task in the now. Do not worry about later but do everything one by one. Consciously choose to stop multitasking.

Your brain is not built to have too many 'programmes' up and running at the same time. In the same way that your computer slows down and starts causing errors when you have too many programmes and documents open at the same time. Continuously trying to accomplish too many tasks at the same time will deplete you. Structure, planning and organization are instruments to create more rest and balance in your life. Mindfulness is another, very useful tool.

*Basic exercises mindfulness: Consciously paying attention to drinking water*

Pour yourself a glass of ice cold water. Observe it for a while and reflect on the origin of the water. In your thoughts trace the way that the water has travelled, through the tap, from the water company, from its natural source, from the air etcetera. Check to see if you can discover bubbles or the way that the water breaks the light.

Now take a small sip of the water. Let the water rest on your tongue and let it roll around in your mouth and note how your mouth reacts naturally to it. Observe your sensations, the taste and the feelings of relief or pleasure that may be associated with the drinking of water. When you swallow the water you may notice the way that your muscles contract and the senses and sounds in your throat and the reaction in your belly. What happens in your mind, what are you thinking and what are the emotions that you experience? Do you want to drink more water? Is your hand moving in the direction of the glass again? Have a few more sips, this way. Pay attention to the reaction of your body and spirit when you swallow the water.

If you repeat this exercise regularly at various times of the day, you will notice different kinds of reactions. Sometimes you will be thirsty or you will feel satisfied. Other times you will feel warm or cold or experience other emotions or physical sensations. If you repeat it every time during the first sips of water it will become a habit after a while and you will be reminded of it automatically, and be transported back to the NOW.

# Chapter 6: Introduce Mindfulness in Your Life

Aside from stopping multitasking, mindfulness offers us even more ways to help us bring more balance in our lives. Mindfulness allows you to abandon your normal, daily patterns and customs: You learn to observe them. You stop for a moment, not to do, but to be. You learn to be present at everything that is happening, at this moment: Unrest, pain, tension, fatigue, anger, joy etc. By not taking immediate action, but remaining calm, you give yourself the chance to familiarise yourself more with your thoughts, your feelings and the sensations in your body. Attention makes you aware of your automatisms, your ingrained thoughts and your repetitive behaviour. This new found awareness offers you a choice: Which thought are you going to invest in and which one will you let be. You are no longer a slave of your own thinking, feeling and doing. This allows you to create freedom, rest and relaxation.

# What is real attention?

The core of mindfulness is learning to do things with utter and complete attention. During the final stages at university, I was mentored by a professor. She counselled more students with their graduation project. She worked on an appointment basis and her appointments were always running late. Something we were not very happy about. This came up during one of our conversations. She told me that she had come to a decision years ago. She could either choose to give each and every student complete attention during the mentor sessions and really dive into what felt important and urgent, or choose to keep an eye on the clock, follow her schedule and remain with the nagging feeling that the students were not getting the best help that she was able and wanted to offer. She chose for the students and to give complete attention.

# Mindfulness and feelings

Feelings such as sorrow, insecurity, lethargy, despair or irritation, can take hold of you and determine your behaviour. If these feelings get too much leeway, they will become stronger. They also have the tendency to reinforce each other, and stack up. What was initially a small cloud, can quickly turn into a raging storm, followed by torrential rains.

From our upbringing we often learn how to deal with feelings in two ways:

- ✓ By suppressing them, feelings can be ignored or lessened. This will not make the feelings disappear, however. They will find other ways to manifest themselves in a different way. For example, via a cynical attitude, forced humour, or through calculated behaviour.

✓ When releasing them, feelings will be fed and enhanced, by talking about them, for example. Or it may be that you wish to dispose of them as soon as possible. Then your feelings will be released via an emotional outburst, complete with all of the unpleasant consequences involved for your immediate environment.

Mindfulness offers a third option to deal with your feelings: you look at them from a distance and allow them to exist simply. You do not feed them; you do not suppress them, and you do not release them, but you allow them to exist without attaching an action to them. Leave the feelings just where they are and resist the impulse to take action.

Then you look at it: When irritated you become aware of the irritation, when happy you experience the happiness, when disappointed and sad you look at the reasons why you feel like that. If you consciously look at it in this way, you create space between you and your feelings. You will notice that the tension of the emotion falls away and within that peace, you will discover that you are not your feelings. You can allow them to exist without getting attached to them; they do not have to determine your mood and your behaviour anymore. You become free at that moment. The following case example is one that is very familiar to me.

Case example:

*"There are days that are so busy at home and everyone in the house is pulling at me. The call of the children can irritate me so much then. Especially at the end of the day when I am cooking and they want anything and everything from me at that moment. I can feel the tension rising in me looking to cause an eruption; "Away with all of you!" I want the pressure to be gone and an emotional outburst like this is the ideal way to unburden myself completely*

*When I did not respond to the situation in this way, something entirely different happened. I felt the outburst rising and for a while I did nothing, I relaxed. I then noticed a space between me and my emotions. And all of a sudden I had to laugh at the immense bustle and chaos that surrounded me, and I was even able to joke about it. The tension was instantly gone and my sense of humour was back. I tend to lose that in the everyday hustle and bustle with the children."*

# Eight important values within mindfulness

Besides focused attention and 'being in the moment', mindfulness is also about having a certain attitude towards life, which helps you experience less stress in daily life. This attitude to life is based on the following eight values. These values are closely knit together and sometimes overlap each other as well.

## I. Do not strive

This is about letting go of the notion of anxiously clinging to the pursuit of all manner of action points and goals. You can set goals, especially if they contribute to your life's happiness, as long as you realise that the path to these aims will be just as it should have been. That the place where you are now, en route to your goals, is exactly the right place for you to be at now.

## II. Do not judge

We are often inclined to judge and have an opinion ready about everything. The funny thing is that we mostly hinder ourselves with all these views and beliefs. The only thing you achieve is more stress. For example, when you believe that you should be capable of many different things, you can ask yourself: why? It is only an opinion, but should you do that?

Or when you are annoyed by another person, ask yourself the following question: Why does this person annoy me? What is in it for me? Should I choose not to be irritated and decide to let go of my judgement? You will start to experience more tranquillity when you do not have to have an opinion on everything anymore.

## III. Open attitude (beginners mind)

Try to approach all of the situations in your life with curiosity. Open yourself up, what does the situation wants you teach you. What lesson can be learned here? What is happening exactly? How does it make me feel? See life, or these situations as something interesting to investigate, instead of something that requires an instant fix or change.

## IV. Let go

Consciously choose to distance yourself from your feelings at times. Be an observer of yourself, experience what your think or feel and let it go in love, you do not need to do anything with it at this time.

## V. Trust

Trust yourself, trust your child and trust life. Know that everything happens for a reason and dare to surrender to the flow of things. Affirmation for yourself: Everything is alright in my world, and I am safe.

## VI. Patience

People sometimes become impatient when they start out with mindfulness, affirmations and meditations. They make steps, they shift their focus and begin to live more from their heart. Even so, the changes they want to achieve can take a little longer to reach. That is part of it. Have patience. Know that you are planting seeds and that the flowers or fruits only appear when the time is right.

## VII. Acceptance

Accept that which is. Change what is within your power or within your 'circle of influence' to modify and accept that which you cannot change. Do not fret about things that you cannot control, nothing costs more energy than that!

## VIII. Compassion

Approach yourself and others with compassion. Every human being does what he or she can with the consciousness of that moment and every person fights his or her own personal battle. Often without us knowing about it. We sometimes judge each other harshly without knowing the whole story. Mindfulness is also about adopting a life attitude based on love and compassion.

# Chapter 7: Teaching Children How to Handle Stimuli

Throughout the day our senses are constantly bombarded with information. All of this information needs to be processed in our minds. Sometimes so much information comes in that it cannot all be processed at once, and this causes stress.

Everyone, children also, have an imaginary bucket. Drops of 'unprocessed information' fall into that bucket. Information that we cannot process immediately. Our buckets are constantly being filled without it being immediately apparent to the outside world. When the bucket is full, there is that last ubiquitous straw which breaks the camel's back. At that moment we become angry, we run away or retreat entirely. Our mind can no longer process all that information and blows a fuse. How quickly a bucket fills up is different in each child. To ensure that your childs bucket does not overflow, he will need time, rest and space to be able to process all of the information. It helps if you as a parent can recognise what it is that is filling your child's bucket.

An example:

*"Danny is playing with Lego with his friend. You can see he is enjoying himself. Suddenly he starts throwing the Lego around the room angrily and bursts into tears, and his mother and his friend stare at him in amazement."*

Something is obviously wrong with Danny, and his outburst appears to be coming out of the blue. But this is not the case. Danny's bucket was full, and something occurred while he was playing, something that for him was the proverbial straw that broke the camel's back, and caused his bucket to overflow.

Observe your child for a while and examine which stimuli your child reacts most strongly to, because if you are aware which stimuli fill your child's bucket faster, you can take this into account and incorporate more rest moments. At the same time you can also consider ways to reduce the input of stimuli, for example one way could be via the use of headphones or sunglasses.

The more stimuli a child has to process, the faster the bucket will fill. The fuller the bucket, means that there is less space for learning, listening and thinking. Knowing what it is that fills your child's bucket, can help prevent undesirable behaviour by overstimulation.

## Mindfulness in the development of our children

Becoming a parent is very challenging. In combination with the high demands set by society, it is not easy to stay calm and be the parent you desperately want to be. Yet, it is worth the effort to do your best to keep calm because the moment you feel zen, you will notice that the days will become more beautiful. That normal moment will regain its shine. You will react in a less agitated way, and you will react less from your mind and more from your intuition. You will restore your appreciation of parenthood, and you will be grateful for it every day.

> An example:
>
> *When the mother gives her son a task, a discussion follows, which leads the son into a temper tantrum. The mother automatically feels angry and helpless and thinks: Why can he not, for once, just do what I ask of him? And: Why do I bother, I can't stand up to him anyway?*
>
> *The mother immediately reacts in a dismissive manner and affirms the child's negative thoughts: I am difficult. Or: My mother does not love me. These repeating child-parent interactions frequently lead to automated thoughts, feelings and conduct that become a habit and are difficult to break.*

When we begin with mindfulness, we see how our spirit is seized by a stream of thoughts, feelings and other perceptions without us being able to get a grip on things, which can influence the quality of our parenting and at times cause stressful situations within the family. We sometimes have the tendency to condemn the behaviour and mindset of our children, and this can lead to tension and irritation.

Mindfulness teaches parents to be acutely aware of the moment itself: With an attitude of not striving and not judging the parental situation at hand. By training our attention, a different way to handle stress and the strain in the parental situation comes into play. As a parent, you learn to raise your children (and their questions and problems) in a non-judgmental and more accepting way, which leads to more peace and balance within the family.

Mindfulness makes you aware of the inner experience of parenting, of your perception of parenting in the here and the now. Mindfulness can also help you improve the emotional experience of your child and his perceptions. You do this by giving attention to your child and your attitude in a special way: deliberately, without judgement and from one moment to the other. This allows you to stay grounded with what is actually important.

Contrary to many parental courses, mindfulness does not offer you quick and concrete educational tips and tricks. Mindfulness is based on the premise that there is no absolute and correct way to raise your children and that no child, no family and no situation is the same. The art is to be flexible, time and again in your reactions to situations as they present themselves. That is why it is important to be constantly aware of your spirit and your own body and the perception of our children. All of this starts with practising our attention.

In some families, a situation of negative interactions between parents and children exists. These are often patterns with a history of conflict and negativity, such as in the case of a mother and her 11-year-old son.

In those cases, mindfulness teaches parents to look consciously at themselves first and then at their child. This causes a change in the parent-child interactions: Perceiving the thoughts and feelings of oneself as mental processes or events, instead of aspects of the person or as an accurate depiction of reality. By looking at this openly and with attention, parents will gain more insight into the interactions between them and their children.

Thanks to a broader view they can often better assess the position of their child and respond more adequately as a result thereof. Compassion with themselves and their child is a specific part of the mindfulness exercise. Parents will react more consciously and are therefore able to break negative patterns.

I have benefitted a great deal from this. Mindfulness has taught me to take a deep breath after one of my children has triggered a reaction from me. By delaying my immediate response and focusing attention on myself, on my feelings and my perceptions, I manage to thwart my automatic response – in my case, explosively raising my voice, or sending of the negative 'you' message – and consciously choose to react in a different, more positive way.

One moment of mindfulness, one moment of attention and compassion for the child and myself, ensures an entirely different outcome. Of course it does not work magically, all of a sudden, but I found it to be a powerful tool, and I became better and better at it!

Mindful parenting ensures more relaxed parents and children. Because let's be fair: Parenting can often cause a lot of stress. Wanting to do well – be the best possible parent – can in itself be a source of stress. The 'hyper-parenting' in which parents believe that the life of their child is realisable and that they have a significant role to play, has gained significant momentum in the last few years. Some parents believe that they have considerable influence regarding their child's self-confidence, of their possibilities regarding building relationships, their success at school and their success in general in social settings. About a third of the parents interviewed believe that they can prevent their child from becoming unhappy. Therefore is isn't at all strange that they feel tremendous pressure to do it 'right'.

There are many challenges and hurdles to overcome, that can make parenting a rather stressful endeavour. To start with, the switch in our lives as adults; from taking care of ourselves to having children and taking care of them, causes an enormous change in the way we divide our time, our attention, our energy, and our inner resources. Life will never be the same after children have been added to the mix.

Taking care of children and organising family life, while trying to balance our professional lives as well, can cause us to neglect ourselves. When our inner resources become depleted, this can lead to an irritable or depressed disposition, as well as fatigue, physical complaints and eventually to psychological or physical ailments that collide with your parental qualities.

Behavioural problems or psychopathology of children and adults are a challenge or barrier that can make parenting that much more stressful. A child can be an extra burden to a family if he becomes stressed or rebellious when confronted with something new. Or when he is unable to play, or organise his homework independently, or cannot be left alone with his siblings due to aggressive conduct or perhaps he cannot sleep at night.

Negative feelings are also frequently felt when trying to combine work and family life. Parents can feel pressured and are often not able to set aside any time for themselves. Some parents recognise the feeling of having too much to do and the sense that they will never be able to finish. Women experience problems more often than men, and women frequently feel that they are on their own, as well as not having any time left for themselves.

According to Bas Levering, pedagogue at the University of Utrecht, small families cause stress mainly for the parents. Small families may seem easier to manage than large families, but nothing could be further from the truth. In larger families, there is less focus on one particular child. The fewer children there are, the more that is expected from them.

# Effects of stress on the family and the parenting style

One of the most challenging aspects of contemporary family life is possibly learning to deal with stress. Stress has a strong negative influence on our style of parenting. When we are tense, we have less attention for our children and ourselves, in relation to our children. Stress causes us to react more impulsively; we become short-tempered and angry, and we worry about the children instead of trusting their growth capabilities.

Parents who have a hard time combining work and family life have a lower sense of wellbeing than those who can easier combine the two. They also experience parenting in a less positive way.

Stress can make educators less effective in two ways. Those who react too sensitively, are easily thrown off balance and need more time to be able to regain this balance. Those who have too many problems can no longer afford to worry about those things which are important for the child. Good parenting is about finding this middle road between too much and too little. Parents who succeed at managing stress well, succeed much better at attaining this balance.

Aside from that, there is substantial evidence that the stress that parents and even grandparents experience, can have an effect on their children and their grandchildren. Obesity or chronic fear can be possible consequences. There is also research that shows that children of parents that have been suffering from stress for longer periods of time, often suffer from fever and a badly functioning immune system. Especially pressure from external sources on the family or stress from psychological illnesses has lots of influence. Lastly, it appears that stress in the family increases the reaction to allergy-causing substances.

This phenomenon can be found in children who suffer from asthma and eczema.

Because of the hustle and bustle of our lives educating sometimes evolves into "managing" children and family, instead of simply being with the children and the family. When this occurs, raising children becomes one of the many tasks on our endless 'to do' list, and we lose sight of the experience of, being in the moment with our children and family. Raising children occurs on autopilot mode, which I was referring to earlier.

When we are stressed, we walk the same negative path with our children, despite our best intentions, because they are the most "ingrained" in our brain. We repeat the same route automatically.

Stress also has a high negative impact on the relationship with your partner. Partners under pressure, frequently have the tendency to start working against each other, rather than to make time for one another, support each other or simply being together. Naturally, when partners have problems in their relationship it directly affects the upbringing situation. When partners do not feel supported by each other, they tend to react more irritated at the children; they withdraw from the children or they become too close to the children, which results in children not receiving enough emotional distance to grow.

No one can prepare you for parenthood, and nobody can help you to always make the right choices. The moment you hold your baby in your arms for the first time, you feel insecure. You are responsible for a little human being. You want to do as best as you can, and you do not always know how. It is easy to lose sight of what is best for your child, while you are trying to provide the best your child. Overwhelmed by the responsibilities, the countless choices and the high expectations, it can cause parenting to lose its lustre. Your head is full; you do not seem to have any time left for anything, and you become irritated. You feel exasperated. You lose the ability to see your children's innocence, or to feel compassion and to stop and reflect. You're wasting the potential to enjoy what may be the most extraordinary journey in your life.

Mindfulness can teach parents to focus their attention better as well as learn them to bring in a certain quality of care. They learn to look at their child in a fresh, non-judgmental way. They also learn to incorporate a moment of attention, during a stressful situation instead of reacting immediately on their child. This makes them see the reality from a broader perspective, which creates more choices in thought and action. Parents learn in this way to better respond to the needs of their child.

## *Aligning to the other*

When parents focus their attention on the inner world of their children, they become attuned to their children. This alignment is the most fundamental way in which the brain activity of parents can influence those of their children, directly.

Child psychiatrist Dan Siegel describes alignment in his book, "The Mindful Brain", as a form of regulation in which developing children use the mental state of their parents to organise their psyche. He examined how mindfulness relates to the neurobiology of a well-aligned parent-child relationship.

Siegel connects the insights of traditional practice with the modern understanding of interpersonal neurobiology. According to him, being attentively aware is a form of inner and outer alignment. His method implies that we connect with others and with ourselves. On the Internet, you can find interesting videos in which he explains his vision.

By giving their children focused attention, parents can help their children develop their brain in a healthy way. Siegel explains that the spiritual state of parents stimulates their children's minds to unite as well. The practice of mindfulness promotes alignment with others by precise observations of emotions and experiences. Several, mindfulness-based games act as a mirror and make sure that we learn better, to see the other person in a funny and entertaining way.

One of these games is a 'reverse follow the leader'. In this game, children are always in command. The idea is that parents do everything the children do, letting them determine the conversations and follow everything in their pace. Without the children discovering that the parents are doing this intentionally. The aim is for parents to feel totally aligned to the rhythm, interests and activities of their children.

Reversing the roles with parents can provide surprising insights into the nature of their children and the way they move through their world. This way parents can experience what it feels like to be their child. Sometimes parents will get even more insight into themselves.

## Practising mindfulness with children

It is a good thing to bring children into contact with mindfulness at an early age. It teaches them to be aware of their inner world (the world of thoughts, feelings and emotions), to observe without immediately judging or responding. Without finding anything weird or stupid, or to put down or push away. Just by peacefully observing the inner world with a friendly and understanding attitude. "What do I feel right now? What do I notice?" It is reassuring to know that there are always thoughts, but you do not always have to listen to them.

Sitting still and being 'in the moment' is one of first basic mindfulness exercises which is a tough thing to do for many children and teenagers. Meditating 'sitting' or 'walking', in silence, can be a major challenge for them. But by doing it regularly, children and teenagers soon learn that to 'sit' and to 'walk' in silence is very calming and soothing.

Practising mindfulness is a skill that children and teens can easily learn, just like learning how to ride a bike, skating or skateboarding. Mindfulness is fun! And for parents, it is nice to be able to practice mindfulness together at home with their children.

We sometimes create a mindful moment during our weekly family meeting. When we notice that our concentration is starting to diminish, we take each other's hand and take three deep breaths while we close our eyes. Breathing is a valuable tool, simply because your breath is always present. You use it to anchor the moment. Kindness is needed to see your patterns clearly and change them if you wish to. You learn by experience. Therefore it is important that you are consciously involved every day. Just as with positive thinking, the act of paying attention to the moment eventually also becomes a habit.

When our children were younger, we often did the following exercise: 'A deep breath before the day begins'. Every family knows the hectic morning ritual - getting everybody out of bed to do the necessary daily tasks like brushing teeth, combing hair and getting dressed. This is in addition to preparing and eating breakfast, together at the table or not, making the lunch boxes, and organising gym bags or any equipment for possible after-school activities. Many families start the day off in this way, and so to improve this experience I have found the following routine to work very well.

When everything and everyone is ready, but before you leave home, everyone will take a pause and collectively takes three deep breaths, together. This means the kids with backpacks on their back, or bags in hand, and the parents with car keys ready for the journey to school and work.

Take several deep breaths in and out to mark the transition from inside to outside, and let your breath transpire quietly to celebrate the moment. All family members will slow down their pace and widen their perspective, before leaving home to greet the new day. This exercise can become a lovely family ritual and an excellent exercise in mindfulness for everyone!

For many families who start practising mindfulness together, the first time can be particularly challenging. Even if the motivation is sincere, there will be times when family members do not want to meditate. That is quite normal. Having the intention to do something is the first step. The challenge is to overcome resistance and then to deal lovingly with yourself and with others. Passion and perseverance are necessary to practice mindfulness and make it into an integral part of family life.

You can keep three guidelines in mind to start with:

## *Keep it simple*

Children are easily distracted. Because of this, parents sometimes tend to add all kinds of bells and whistles to an activity or a game to keep the children captivated. Experience shows that the simplest of exercises often have the greatest impact and are often the most attractive to children.

## *Keep it fun*

It is nearly impossible to concentrate when you are hungry or tired, and it is no fun at all. The link between food and attention is often overlooked. Eating a healthy snack before the mindfulness session begins helps children to concentrate better. A similar relationship exists between sleep and attention, and between stress and attention. Nowadays many children experience stress at a young age. This is partly due to the increasing pressure on (young) children because of tests, quizzes and a multitude of necessary activities. When was the last time your child had absolutely nothing to do in the afternoon?

Fatigue, hunger and being overburdened bring about a substantial disadvantage within the framework of mindfulness (not to mention health- and developmental problems that can develop as a result of the above); it narrows our outlook. It diminishes our ability to look at our lives, clearly and objectively. More importantly, they no longer have fun. Children have to be well rested and well fed to be able to concentrate and to learn.

## *Maintain your sense of humour*

First of all, it is important to keep in mind that children can make it tough for you when you are asking them to pay attention, when you are not.

Secondly, you must first experience what mindfulness means for yourself or what meditation does to you before you can transfer this knowledge to children in a credible and enthusiastic manner. Never try to do something you have not experienced yet. Children will sense that something is not real.

## Important lessons and insights from Part 3

### For yourself

- ✓ The information overload was never as high as it is now; for yourself as well as for your children.

- ✓ Multitasking leads to unrest, stress and an unfulfilled feeling; it is much better to do things one by one.

- ✓ Many of our daily actions and thoughts happen on automatic pilot; you do them without thinking about them because patterns that have been created.

- ✓ Mindfulness offers a moment of rest between action and reaction; you can consciously choose how to react to the situation.

- ✓ Mindfulness provides very important values, such as letting go of judgement, developing a 'beginner's mind', letting go, trust, the cultivation of patience and compassion.

### In relation to your child(ren)

- ✓ Children can become overstimulated by all the stimuli they receive during the day.

- ✓ Mindful upbringing can end stress and a negative atmosphere in a home because it teaches you to act from a place of peace and confidence, in parental situations as well as with your children.

- ✓ Mindfulness helps you align yourself better with your child(ren's) world, and with their experiences and emotions; it improves the relationship and stimulates the development of their brain.

✓ Practising mindfulness meditation together is fun and a matter of practice and sticking to it.

In this third part, you were provided with tips on how to live 'in the moment', on how to silence that critical voice in your head and on how to handle your daily affairs consciously. To aid you and your children with this, I have five beautiful colouring pages of mandalas with powerful and positive affirmations for you for both younger and older children. Even my teenagers love this! To gain access to this creative gift, go to: www.nolimitparenting.com/bonuses or scan this QR-code

# Part 4

## Have the COURAGE to follow your heart: Find your passion

*Passion is energy. Feel the power that comes from focusing on what excites you.*

*- Oprah Winfrey*

# Follow Your Heart and Encourage Your Children to Discover Their Path

If you are aware of what values are important to you, as a person and as a family, and what your purpose is in this world, you will give yourself and your kids a strong inner compass. If you know what is crucial in your child's upbringing, in your work and your life, then making the right choices becomes much easier. If your mission is clear to you, your life becomes simpler; and you will start living from your fundamental values.

Find your passion, follow your heart. I know it might sound like the latest craze. Suddenly we all want to find our passion and live life from our hearts. Yet still, I believe that life exists for this reason: Do that what makes you happy, something that makes you feel that what you are doing makes sense. Our intention should be about bringing our unique talents and love into the world, and that the world will become a better place for it. If we keep doing what we think others expect from us, instead of following our hearts, I truly believe that we miss the whole point of what life is all about.

Many people live their lives without really thinking about it. They do what others expect of them, following the path that their environment or society has marked out for them. They go to work every day to a job that neither challenges nor inspire them. A job in which they may, or cannot, show all of their abilities. Without even realising it, they postpone their needs or desires until later. They spend much of their time doing things they do not care about because they believe that this is what is expected of them.

Research indicates that we only use around 10% of our brain capacity, and thus of our opportunities. But I would so much love to know who you really are! The world wants to know your greatness.

Who are you? What is it that can get you to literally jump out of bed in the morning. What are your wildest dreams? Do not let the fear that is perhaps now stirring in you, stop you. Be brave! Speak up, shout out to the world. What is it that makes your heart beat faster?

> *If your dream doesn't scare you, it is not big enough.*

Do you recognise that gnawing feeling you have that you are meant for bigger things? That life was not intended to be about paying bills each month, to work at a job where you cannot make a difference, and to lose so much energy, worrying about everyday concerns, just to survive?

I'm sure have a burning desire to make your life more meaningful. The feeling that you want to matter, that you want to create a different life for yourself and that you are looking to deepen the relationships with your loved ones and yourself. Somewhere inside of you, you feel that this is possible. You know it, intuitively.

But then your ego takes over again; the voices in your head try to steer you off your path and fear grabs you by the throat. The voices in your head say things like: "Now is not the right time" or "I don't have enough money", etcetera. That I also know.

From personal experience I know that your intuition is always right. You too can live a great life. It is possible. Time and again people have risen beyond their limitations to accomplish extraordinary things. Nelson Mandela, Beethoven, Shakespeare, Barak Obama, or whomever you admire. These are people just like you and me.

Every dream, however large or small, begins with a thought, an idea. So dare to dream!

I promise you that the freedom it grants you to abandon the beaten track, to extend your boundaries and to step into your greatness, will give you an amazing feeling, and it is excellent for confidence building.

Please avoid the pitfalls of victimhood. We are so quick to think that real freedom and affluence is not meant for us. We believe that we are victims because of our origins, our traumas and our formal training. Let me tell you: You are not a victim. You are a beautiful human being with unique talents and abilities, and with an indescribable amount of love in your heart.

So start looking for YOUR passion!

This can be pretty scary, and you will need to overcome some hurdles, but if you dare, it will give you great satisfaction. And what I have experienced myself is that it always works out in the end! Once you dare to follow your heart, everything starts to flow more in your life. Everything seems to come together, and practical problems tend to solve themselves.

There is something to be learnt with every step you take. My most valuable lessons on this path thus far have been:

- ✓ More is not necessarily better.

- ✓ There is no 'one best way'.

- ✓ It does not have to be perfect (whatever it may be).

- ✓ I can change my course if that feels better.

# Chapter 8: In Search of Your Passion

The word 'passion' does not trigger a reaction in everybody. But this isn't necessary. Other people feel more at ease with words like 'inspiration', 'energy', and that which makes you 'happy'. It is all good! Use the word that expresses your feelings best.

## *What is a passion?*

I read somewhere that passion is ardour, a journey through the heart. I found it to be a beautiful description. It is important to note that passion is not only that which you do but mainly that which you are. This forms an excellent link with the previous chapter about mindfulness, where the shift from DOING to BEING is the central theme. There is passion in everyone; it is the core of your BEING

Passion is always there. It may not have been granted any space through the years, so it has probably been pushed to the background. Yet, it is possible to rekindle long forgotten desires and forces.

An Exercise:

Ask 10 people in your environment (family, friends, and colleagues) if they can name 3 qualities or talents you possess. Write them all down, and turn them into a word cloud on your computer, or make a collage of them. Look at the words, search for a common thread and let it sink in. Think about how you want to best commit all of these qualities.

To get closer to your passion, you need to answer the three following questions:

## A. What are important values for you?

In Part 2 we talked about the importance of values and knowing your personal values. Values are input for your 'why'. What do you believe in? Why do you do what you do? If you are aware of what you stand for, you will inspire yourself and others.

There are many values of which almost everyone will say YES to, but you have to feel them strongly. Your heart must skip a beat, and you must feel deep inside: This is what I want, this is who I want to be, and this is what I want to radiate.

Take honesty for example. Everyone thinks this is an important value. But does this value make your heart skip a beat, deep down inside? What do you wish to achieve? How do you want to be remembered later, by your children, your colleague's and your partner?

## B. What are your most important qualities?

People often find it difficult to identify and acknowledge their strengths. If we are good at something, we believe it to be quite 'normal' that we can do it well, we do not recognise it as a talent or strenght. In addition to identifying your qualities, acknowledging them is also paramount. People think too quickly that they are somehow not good at something if they know others who are slightly better at the same thing. We love to compare ourselves with others. If you acknowledge that everyone has unique talents and passions, it might be a lot easier to see and appreciate your personal strengths.

## C. What makes you happy, what do you dream of?

What do you like to do? Which activities did you enjoy doing most when you were a child? At what moment do you forget about time? What is it that causes your heart to glow? What is it that you would love to do most if you did not have to worry about money, time or other practical constraints?

My motivation has always been wanting to teach others. I have always wanted to share the lessons I had learnt at school with my loved ones. And how incredible it is, to realise that this is still what I love to do most of all: To share my knowledge and my experience with others. I love to inspire others and share my successes and experiences. And furthermore: From the bottom of my heart, I hope that others will go and use my knowledge to their advantage! That the others will realise: "If Monique can do that, then maybe I can do that too!" That is my hope for you. That the flame within you will be rekindled again and that it will fuel a beautiful burning desire. Because that desire is the engine that will create your dream life.

Some people do not dare to dream. That always makes me very sad. This is your life. Love yourself fully and please dare to dream. You can manifest anything that you dare to dream. And getting in touch with your dreams, desires and your passion is the catalyst you need to achieve them. Do not let fear hold you back, your courage will be rewarded.

Finding your passion is all about the unique message you want to put out into the world. If you had a magic wand, what would you most want to change or improve? And why?

When it comes to finding and following our passion, we often wait for permission or approval from others. We think we need to work very hard to be allowed to live in abundance. Or we believe that true wealth, true love and true happiness are things that are not intended for us.

However, doing what you really want to do and having your dreams come true, is mainly a matter of giving yourself permission. No one else will do this for you. The blockade frequently lies in feelings of shame and guilt, incurred somewhere during your life.

According to Benjamin Harvey, your greatness lies hidden in your most embarrassing moments. So ask yourself, "How can I use this experience or shape it into my higher mission to serve others in this world?" "How can I mould my biggest challenges into greatness?"

The underlying question is: What makes me really happy? For me it is writing, inspiring people, reflecting on the madness and beauty of life, a good conversation with one of my children, a close friend or my husband. These are the moments that make me feel extremely grateful, enthusiastic and happy.

Yet, we often do not spend enough time on activities that make us truly happy. Why is it that we frequently spend so little time on the really important things, while we stand and proclaim that we would like to do other things? Thinking that we do not have time for it or are not ready for it. First, we must do this and do that, and then we will do what we actually want to do. Strange.

I have come to discover that behind this procrastinating behaviour, a great fear lies hidden. Yes, fear. I was actually scared to death of spending more time on things that were important to me. And fulfilling the fear of making other choices held me back for years.

## Fear of not being good enough

Can I write well enough? Can I coach well enough? Am I in any way inspiring enough for others? Am I good enough? These are essential questions that only you can answer.

The more you can accept yourself and approve of yourself, the more you can say, with conviction: I am good enough. We frequently seek the approval of others, but in reality, that nagging inner voice only really goes away when you can give yourself that approval.

## Fear of sharing your story

We often think that we are alone with our concerns, our problems and wild ideas. Me too. Others will think I am childish, or emotional, or unprofessional. Oddly enough, you will notice that when you share these "wild ideas" with others, you learn that they have them too. Sometimes they may have even "crazier" beliefs or concerns. Which is why it is really great to share these things with one another.

But it remains "scary" because it makes you vulnerable (or at least that is how it feels), when you share what is happening in your inner world, with the outside world. Especially if you are not accustomed to do so. But there are so many people, both in the virtual and the real world that can inspire and encourage you. Just by telling their own story; why would my or your story not have that same strength for others?

## Fear of financial insecurity

Many people think that - if they decide to only do what they like - they will inevitably end up knee-deep in financial peril. At this point in my life, I have already amassed sufficient evidence to prove that if you do that which makes you genuinely happy and truly gets you going, then the money will start pouring in. Indeed, just rush headfirst and realise your dreams, without fears. Money will be available, one way or the other, to help you achieve your dreams. The universe will reward you for your courage. It will always work out in the end.

The important thing when connecting to your deepest desires is that it will all become clear to you. That you have a clear picture of how it would be to do that, which you wish to do more than anything in the world and how that would feel. Be completely WILD when you are thinking about what you would want to do and how you would want to live. Give yourself absolute FREEDOM!

They do not have to be grand things or piles of money and material things because small changes can also hide great desires. Feel the butterflies in your belly when you write down your dreams. They are a sign that you are on the right track. Answer the following questions afterwards. Do this on a clean sheet of paper where you can write freely or use as a mind map by jotting down everything that comes to mind. Do not think too long, and give your thoughts free reign and let the answers flow naturally.

---

If I had no fear and would not hinder myself, and if I did not have to worry about money and time, and if I was completely free, then ...

I would want to do this: ... ... ... ... ... ... ... ... ... ... ... ... ... ...

I would want to have this: ... ... ... ... ... ... ... ... ... ... ... ... ...

I would want to be here: ... ... ... ... ... ... ... ... ... ... ... ... ... ...

I would like to be surrounded by these people:

I would like to earn this amount of money every month: ... ...

I would like to contribute this to the world ... ... ... ... ... ...

I would like to live like this:   ... ... ... ... ... ... ... ... ... ... ... ...

I would like to create this:  ... ... ... ... ... ... ... ... ... ... ... ... ...

I would then feel like this:  ... ... ... ... ... ... ... ... ... ... ... ... ...

Let go of your fears and you will discover that true happiness is there for the taking. Face your fears and go and do more of what makes you happy! No matter how small the first step is, start now. Nobody is ever completely ready for whatever can be. There is never a perfect moment for whatever can be. NOW is good enough.

## *From fear to love*

The way I conquer my fears is to focus on love. I know how fear can drive you away from your passion and your dreams. For a long time, for me, the fear of lack of money held me back. Even though I had never suffered from a lack of food, over time I had somehow developed a line of thinking based on poverty and scarcity. During the years 2010-2012, we went through a financial rough patch. I remember waking up in the middle of the night and feeling genuine panic. Complete with heart palpitations and cold sweats. I could not rationally explain the source of my fear, except that it had to do with our financial situation. I blamed myself and felt like a failure. Only now do I realise that one's bank balance is a reflection of self-worth. The value which you give to yourself. Of the love that you feel for yourself.

The more I started to love myself and the more I started thinking in abundance, the more money started flowing into my life.

Another fear that I know all too well is the one I always experience when I decide to step out of my comfort zone. I was shaking like a leaf for example when I signed the contract for an online programme that would help me with the publishing process involved with this book. For me, this was a moment that I had made the decision to finally write this book in which I wanted to share my message with thousands of people. I now know that this nervous feeling somewhere in the middle of your body – just below your sternum, also called the Plexus Solaris and part of the random nervous system – means that you are growing. That you are taking the next step in your development. That it is a great feeling. Earlier in my life, though, I have at times let this feeling that I called fear stop me from doing what I wanted to do.

Fear is the most fundamental of all our negative emotions; it is one extreme of the spectrum love – fear. All problems, feelings and pain stem from that one primordial feeling: Fear. Fear is intangible and more often than not, unrealistic and unfounded. And yet there it is. Fear is the absence of love. Love is, therefore, the best answer to fear. Love melts everything, even fear. Self-love, love for others and love of life. Introduce more love into your life, and your fears will diminish.

## *How can you deal with fear?*

The first step is realising that you have fear and that you are not fear. This creates a certain distance, as it were, from which you can face your fears head-on. The next step is to start to acknowledge and accept your fears. Fear is permitted: name what it is exactly that you are afraid of. Another good exercise is to repeatedly ask yourself "Why?"

Start off with saying: 'I am afraid of … Or because … '

Then ask yourself: 'Why?'

Write your answer down and ask yourself again: 'Why?'

Repeat this five times and in many cases, you will have reached a reply to the core of fear.

You can now thank your fear because fear always has a purpose. Acknowledge fear as a friend who has protected you from something that was too painful or too difficult at the time. Thank your fear for protecting you. Send it love and affirm: it is now safe for me to release my fear. I am safe.

The fourth step is to make the decision to not let your fear take over your life anymore. It is not your fear that controls your life, it is you! As I explained earlier in chapter 2, there is great power that comes from a firm resolve in making a conscious choice. The moment you make this decision it is already in effect. Everything in the universe will adjust itself the minute you consciously make a decision.

Finally, you become aware of your capabilities, of the infinite potential that you possess, as soon as you let go of your fears. You are allowed to focus all your energy to yourself. You can now try to love yourself as you love your children, or your family and friends. Be aware of your value in the world, replace your fears with love.

During anxious moments in my life, I always repeat my base affirmation: "I love and accept myself." This restores my peace and helps me to release my fears. The time it takes to make this shift from fear to love, is different for everyone. It depends on how deeply rooted your fear is, and certain events in your life can also affect your sense of fear. In any case, 'the inner work must be done'.

Fear is the emotion of loathing, of isolation, of flying, of rejection, of jealousy, of envy and of all other negative feelings. Love is the emotion of embracing, of being together, of happiness and of all other positive emotions. In every situation in your life, you react mainly from one of these two emotions. You act from love or from fear.

You must realise that fear is allowed and has had a purpose in your life. It might seem incredible to experience only love and never again fear. Unfortunately (or fortunately) that is impossible. Although fear and love seem to be two very different feelings, you will discover that they are inseparable, just as two sides of a coin.

As long as you do not want to experience fear, you will never experience true love. Of course this does not mean that you will immediately experience love when you feel anxious. It means that there is a possibility to not resist the feeling of fear. To allow that sensation to be there as long as it lasts, and if you grab the chance, you will experience love, against all odds.

Welcoming the feeling of fear isn't pleasant. Most people want to get rid of it as soon as possible. We do this in several ways. By putting it into perspective, by denigration, irritation, by avoiding it, by trying to explain it, by finding solutions, by eating, by drinking, watching TV, by working, helping, etc. We will do anything and everything so that we do not have to experience that feeling. And it even seems to work as well. However, the downside is that if you do not want to feel fear in your body, you will not feel the love!

Avoiding and pushing away feelings of fear leads to numbness, and loss of emotions. If you avoid fear at all cost, after some time (usually after many years), the lack of love will be so great that you will not know what to do anymore. You cannot understand why it does not feel right on the inside, even though things appear to be going well. You do not want to continue in this way, but you dare not accept change. If that happens, then that is your big opportunity. Fear presents itself again. And the feeling of fear is becoming clearer.

This is your chance to experience fear, entirely voluntarily. What am I afraid of and what is the exact feeling in my body? How long does last it when I invite the feeling to stay in my body? Can I use real honesty and voice it? How does that feel? Then you start to feel again. First the fear, the precursor of love and freedom. Then love and freedom itself.

Many people react out of fear automatically. They are afraid of losing something or experiencing something that they do not want to. But you have the choice to determine which emotion you wish to react from. So with each choice, ask yourself this: what would I love to do now? It will help you make decisions based on love so that fear will no longer rule your life!

# Chapter 9: Bringing Children into Contact with Their Inner Power

The next step is to consider how we can encourage our children to find their own way in life. Children are very imaginative and creative and masters at seeking solutions to their problems. Young children especially are very open-minded and tend to see beauty and goodness in everything. They are born with the ability to ask, to dream and to wonder. Everything is possible, and that is good.

As children get older, they become more aware of their identity and start thinking about how they come across to others and what others may think of them, this can hinder creativity. Our school system and education, in general, are also often not focused on fostering and promoting this innate creativity. Unfortunately, children soon learn to adapt to the beaten path and standard solutions. The out-of-the-box thinking disappears quickly.

Children's education is often focused on conformism: Do what the rest does and stay in line. In the beautiful film "Dead Poets Society," with a sublime role by the late Robin Williams as an unorthodox English teacher, visualised this to the extreme in the picture. The story takes place in an elite boarding school of Welton Academy, 1959. One of the students discovers his passion for drama and he shines in his role in the play 'A Midsummer Night's Dream'. His love for the stage fully coincides with who he wants to be and what he intends to do for the rest of his life. When his father discovers that he has applied for a part in this play and learned that his son has aspirations to become an actor, he threatens to send him to a military school, and then to Harvard to become a doctor. Neil lacks the courage to face his father and commits suicide. Not being able to, or not being allowed to follow your heart, or not being able to express your creativity is painful. It can even be intolerable.

Creativity still gets far too little attention in the formation and education of our children. To nurture creativity in children, it is necessary that adults encourage them to stay explorers and to follow their dreams.

## *Stimulation of creativity*

Creative education is very limited in most schools. Pre-schoolers mostly learn to cut and paste things by their teachers example. In fact, schools teach children mainly to 'colour within the lines', i.e. learn a high degree of conformity, and it does not end there.

On the soccer field and other sporting arenas, children are primarily taught to cater to the tight rules that adults have invented. While strategic insight and sportsmanship in general are important values, it still doesn't encourage and nurture creative behaviour in children.

This is regrettable because creativity entails so much more than exercises in dexterity. Creativity is essentially about encouraging children to find the path that suits their personality, about giving them confidence and about finding new solutions. It is about doing something that excites you. And it is also about persevering, even if those around you think your plan is weird or stupid.

The movie "The Pursuit of Happiness" – based on the book with the same title – tells a true story of Chris Gardner, a father who, despite various setbacks, tries to find happiness and attempts to realise a good life for his son. Chris, played by Will Smith, is so determined to achieve his dream, that he (after his girlfriend and the mother of his son has left them) registers for a six-month unpaid traineeship. His financial situation becomes so uncertain, that he and his son are even forced to sleep in a public bathroom of a subway station at one point. In one moment during the movie he makes a brilliant statement that really touched me; he tells his son:

*"Don't ever let someone tell you that you can't do something. Not even me. You got a dream; you gotta protect it. When people can't*

*do something themselves, they're gonna tell you that you can't do it. You want something, go get it. Period."*

He says this at a moment when he is discouraging his son from playing basketball, and this is something I think we all know. Your children share their dreams with you – I want to be a famous basketball player – and in that moment you experience just how challenging life can be. Before you know it, you shatter that dream with a downplayed remark like: "That is a long road, though, it is only reserved for the very best basketball players, and you will have to train for a very long time." In that one small moment, your child can decide to give up his dream. Fortunately, Chris Gardner realises this in time.

Creativity often seems to be the unique aptitude of only a few people. But in fact, we are all born with the talent to be creative; what happens to this sixth sense as we grow older?

Too often it remains dormant, or dreams are, slowly but surely, extinguished. Fortunately, this is changing. A creative personality is no longer solely associated with art; science, sports and the business world are also in need of creative people.

You can encourage your child's artistic talent by taking seriously his ability to enrich life emotionally, and by stimulating their creative side. The key here is to grant children room to be themselves.

As much as possible, give children the freedom to do things their way. Maybe you will not understand everything, but it will give them something extremely valuable: satisfying their ego and strengthening their self-confidence.

An example: two children argue over how many large blocks each of them can have. Billy holds one of his blocks above his head and says, "I will hit you if you do not give me more!" The children continue to argue until Timmy reluctantly says at one point: "Okay, I will give you more." "How many?" asks Bill. "A hundred," Timmy replies.

At this point, you may be wondering where Timmy is going to get a hundred blocks. Timmy starts counting aloud as he hands over to Billy Blocks: "One, two, three, seventy, forty, forty-five, and a hundred." Billy takes the seven blocks, smiles and starts to build together with Timmy.

Billy and Timmy teach us that we need to let children use their power of imagination to solve problems, in their own way. Creativity flows smoothly in children as they approach situations without too many preconceived ideas.

They come up with different ways to solve simple problems, and sometimes they have the wildest ideas. But if children learn, at an early age, that they will receive praise when they adapt, then they will do so.

Disapproving this uniqueness will make children stop trying to be extraordinary. Parents also teach children not to be original when they make comments like, "Why can't you be a little more like your nephew?" When we compare a child with other children, he learns that it is better to imitate someone else, rather than being himself.

There are creative children who do hold on to their originality, though, despite of everything that life throws at them. Ideas come to them like rockets, not as a means to earn praise or money, but because of the inner joy they find in creation. Unless a family gives these children the consideration they need, this kind of individualistic behaviour can cause problems between parents and children, instead of it leading to intense joy.

Parents can use their creative talents to encourage their children to develop creativity. To solve the problems of the harsh world they face, kids will have to rely on their originality. Creativity is a life force that can lead us to lead a happy and prosperous life.

Parents want to give their children everything; Karate lessons, guitar and ballet lessons, scouting and other clubs, you name it. It seems that we need to fill every single moment of the week with activities. Of course, it is necessary and fun to be active, but more often than not, an overstimulated child does not have an excessive need for action, but rather a moment to contemplate things. Peaceful moments stimulate imagination. How can you find the time to dream when the there is so little of it, and daydreaming seems forbidden? Daydreaming leads to creativity. "Go to your room!" A statement like this can sound like music to the ears of a rebellious child, because it may be the only chance for him or her to be alone, stretch out on the bed or lie on the floor, dreaming or reading a book (which is, in essence, someone else's dream put to words).

All in all, it is about allowing a creative and "no limit parenting" to encourage children to experiment and find their personal style and passions. As parents, you are an intrinsic part of the process.

Wayne Dyer, in his book "What do you really want for your children?" hands us some strategies, such as the following:

1. Allow children to learn from their own perspective. This means that parents must maintain a patient attitude and allow children to discover their own possibilities. Allow children the opportunity to explore what it is that they want to do in life.

2.  Creativity and taking risks go hand in hand. Allow children space to experiment. Let them come up with their own recipes, create their own contraptions or their own game. Take the pressure of an organised life away and allow as much spontaneity as possible.

3.  Let children be themselves in as many aspects of their lives as possible. Let them define their own rules and do not spoon-feed everything for them. Creative people never stay within the borders during their lives. They do everything their own way.

4.  Give children praise for their own style. Suppress any urge to compare children with others.

5.  Take children seriously. A child is not a human being that is 'unfinished', but a complete person with his or her own possibilities on his or her own developmental level.

6.  Do not quote rules as a reason for children to have to do something. A creative approach to life entails that you make your own decisions on almost everything that you do.

7.  Show that there are many different perspectives on how to approach an issue and that there are, more often than not, no right or wrong answers. Are people in rich countries happier than people in poorer countries? That is debatable. Do not be afraid to say that you do not know something and teach your children those same words too. Creative people become motivated and engage in research, by these words.

8.  Creative people need privacy. The same is valid for children. Allow them their own space, where they can withdraw and do what pleases them at that moment.

9.  Creative people do creative work in the first place because they derive pleasure and satisfaction from it. Not because of rewards such as salary, prizes or praise. When you praise a child, try to emphasise what it means to them personally, and do not teach them to strive for external (good grades, compliments, presents) rewards external rewards can undermine, the so-called 'intrinsic gain' entirely, as has been shown in psychological experiments. If it becomes a 'must' because of one reason or the other, then it no longer provides any satisfaction.

10. There is nothing at all wrong with boredom. It does not always have to be fun. Frustration teaches children far more than a life wherein every step is mapped out and they do not carry any responsibility themselves.

*"The purpose of education is to replace an empty mind with an open one."*

*Malcolm Forbes*

The best thing you can do in addition to this is to lead by example. Live your dreams and try to be your real self every time. Be genuine and be true to yourself. Oddly enough, this is something that we often find very difficult to do.

What is it that causes us not to be completely empowered, and what can we do to ensure that we become 'more ourselves'? Often, it is our personal obstructive convictions that hinder us from 'showing our real face' to the world :

✓ We are afraid of not being accepted or not belonging if we just are who we are.

✓ We fear that we are not good enough to do the things that we would love to do most of all, or that there are others that are much better at it.

✓ We do not wish to attract attention to ourselves, or think that others might think us to be pretentious; we do not want others to think that our ambitions have 'gone to our heads'.

✓ We fear to shine and show the world how powerful and beautiful we really are.

✓     ... ... ... (you fill in!) > What is holding you back?

**Get to know yourself and let yourself be seen!**

The greatest confusion that arises when mentioning 'becoming yourself' is that people assume that there is something to be discovered. This is simply not the case. It is more a matter of becoming 'more' of what is already there. Because of the fears above and convictions it often requires courage to be yourself, to not adapt yourself too much to the societal standards or continuously aligning yourself with other people's expectations of you. Have the courage to be who you are and have the courage to fail. Loosen up!

Do not worry about the worst thing that could happen, especially in social situations. Life just goes on even when you blunder, even if there is a bit of spinach stuck between your teeth, or you accidentally bump your head! Learn to laugh at yourself, not only the moment it happens, but afterwards as well. Think about what is necessary to handle certain situations with courage. Make a story of it that you can share with others. It shows them that you are not perfect. It is an attractive quality, to be able to laugh at oneself. Do not take yourself too seriously!

## Creativity, self-confidence and resiliency

Every child has his or her unique talents. Stimulate children to discover which talents they are and do not think too much regarding right and wrong. If a child regularly hears that his attempts are not good enough or that he has to do things differently, he will stop that behaviour in the end. It is important to give children room to discover and grow.

It is also important to name and appreciate all of their talents. We often add value to cognitive abilities (the child gets good grades at school) but do express your appreciation for the less straightforward skills and qualities, such as empathy, helpfulness, patience, a rich imagination, able to console others well, good at handicrafts and able to play well together.

You can teach them to how to stand firm so that they know who they are and the things they stand for. This way they can make choices that are right for them and others. Children are always busy discovering who they are. This is a trial and error process that grows throughout the various age phases. Knowing who you are and accepting who you are essential building blocks for building resiliency. It ensures that you dare to stand up for yourself because you know that you are worth it.

There is a strong connection between resiliency and self-confidence. A child that is self-confident dares to stand up for himself and is resilient. Children with little confidence and who are not resilient are likely to be bullied or can easily be (negatively) influenced by other children. For example, joining in the bullying of other children or the use of swear words, because their friend does the same.

Next to stimulating creativity and originality, encouraging resilience is, therefore, important as well, so that your child can stand up for the things that he or she wants. There is a strong connection between self-confidence and resilience, which is what chapter 1 was all about.

It also helps to give children responsibilities. Being able to solve problems themselves is an important skill for both the resilience and for the self-confidence of the child. But my, don't we love solving our children's problems? In addition to this, we often want to ward off problems in advance from our children. In this way, we deprive them of the possibility to handle and resolve any issues and limit their opportunity to develop a greater self-confidence. If we demand too little of our children and constantly spoon-feed ideas, we can also help nurture a negative self-image. These children may feel that parents think they cannot do anything independently.

It is important for a child to learn how to deal with frustrations, and occasionally he must also be confronted with things that go wrong or different than he expected. A resilient child has a degree of frustration tolerance; he is then able to cope when things do not go as planned. Children can only learn these things by encountering setbacks and learning how to cope with them.

## *Involve your children in your work!*

In my experience you can subconsciously give the right example by doing what you like to do the most. I have discovered that by being an entrepreneur and working from home, your children unknowingly gather a lot of what you are doing. All my four children came away with something else from this example.

My nine year old is mostly impressed by the message that I wish to spread through my work. That message is, that everything in your life is a reflection of your personal mindset and how this is your full responsibility. Whenever I cry out, "But that is way too expensive!" or, "We cannot afford that now", he elegantly reminds me: "Mom, you do know thoughts are forces right? Money will flow to us!" When I express that I am having a bad day, he says: "You chose that yourself, you can also decide to have a great day!"

My second child, my 11-year-old son, watches YouTube, all day. He searches for everything on YouTube; from 'how to bake the most delicious brownies' to 'how to make a bow and arrow' or 'what to do when you forget your iPhone password' to 'how to make a fire when you have to survive in the jungle'.

Ever since he saw me busy making video's for my free video course and online programme, he developed a taste for it. He set up a YouTube channel and now regularly needs to borrow my phone, because he needs to make a short film for his YouTube account. And so he takes his viewers on an adventure to his hut, which is close to our home. He demonstrates what happens when you eat a fresh red hot pepper, or he shares his admiration when he discovers an exceptional Australian bird. He keeps close tabs on how many subscribers he has. As his mother, I watch and listen in amazement how he narrates these films in fluent English.

Son number three, who is 13 years old, is interested in all aspects of money making. He sees opportunities everywhere and seizes every opportunity to make deals. He thinks that it is funny that his mother, being an online entrepreneur and engaged in all forms of technology, now turns to him for tips and advice. It was no trouble for him at all to edit my video's for my video course either. To my surprise and enthusiasm, he managed to incorporate slides into my amateurish recorded video's and added music tracks to my narrated meditations and visualisations. He managed to make me look really professional!

Then there is my 17-year-old daughter. When we still lived in Curacao, she surprised us with her website, entitled, 'Babysitting with love', which she made one afternoon for her job as a babysitter. The website was complete with references, diplomas, pictures and a contact page. I had been struggling for months to build my website! Of course, she had also made a business Facebook page and soon she was earning a nice bit of extra money from this. A very useful thing for this passionate Apple fan who wants to buy all the latest gadgets.

When we had just arrived in Sydney, Australia she complained: "How will I come by new babysitting addresses?". However, again she quickly took a very focused approach to this, by translating her website in English and posting messages on Facebook in groups such as 'Dutchmen in Sydney' and also asked me to share her posts. And wouldn't you know it, my daughter found three new families to babysit for in no time at all! In the meantime she now baby-sits for more families and also works part-time in a café.

One night I was really flabbergasted. After I had finished an inspiring Skype session with a fellow entrepreneur, in which we were attempting to boost each other to take the next step, my daughter came to me: "Mum, come here I want to show you something."

She was about to order business cards online, and she asked me what I thought of the design. Of course, she had designed them herself. "They are beautiful", I replied sincerely. "All right, can I borrow your credit card then, because I am going to order them. I'll pay you back in cash." She entered all the necessary data and asked me to check the last page before she pressed the 'Place order' button. I noticed that she had ordered a card holder as well ("At least then your cards will stay neat", she chatted cheerfully) and I noticed that there were shipping charges involved as well. "Amber, are you sure?" I inquired carefully. "You will have spent all of your money". She looked at me with a smile and said: "Yes Mum, that is doing business, isn't it? You have to invest in your company!"

## Important lessons and insights from Part 4

## For yourself

- ✓ I believe that you are here on this earth to share your unique talents and qualities with others, in such a way that completely befits you.

- ✓ Everybody has passion; it is the core of who you are

- ✓ Passion is that area where your values coincide with your qualities

- ✓ The most important thing that you can do for yourself is to give yourself permission to start following your heart and living your passion

- ✓ When you do not allow your fears to hold you back, you will experience an enormous feeling of freedom and happiness

## In relation to your child(ren)

- ✓ Stimulate the natural creativity in your child(ren)

- ✓ Stimulate the uniqueness in your child(ren) and give them the courage to be who they are.

- ✓ Give the right example, show them that your work is not a 'must' but that it gives you pleasure and satisfaction

In Part 4, I write about finding your passion, which can be quite the challenge. Aside from making a 'vision or mood board', creating a mind-map can also be a useful tool to gain more insight into your talents and passions. I explain how in the 'Passion Mindmap'. Mindmaps are often used in the educational system, so your children will most likely be able to help you out, or better yet, let them make their own 'Passion Mindmap'!

To gain access to this helpful gift, go to: www.nolimitparenting.com/bonuses or scan this QR-code.

# Part 5

## Use loving and positive COMMUNICATION (Watch your language)

*Seek first to understand. Then to be understood*

~ Stephen Covey

# Learn to Communicate Lovingly and Effectively to Establish a Better Relationship with Your Children

Learning to communicate effectively is the most important ability in life. Communication is a fundamental thing in any relationship, whether it is about communication with your partner, your child, your boss, your colleague or your mother. I could emphasise it even more by stating: Relationship = Communication. To this end, we use words, gestures and facial expressions. It seems that most people have approximately 60,000 words in their vocabulary at their disposition. In closer examination, they often use them in a random, careless, forceful or indirect manner. We all know how it feels to become irritated or disappointed because we think that others don't 'want' to understand what we are saying. Things that are so obvious to us. Often, in conversation, we quickly assume that others know what we mean. This is a bad strategy. How can that be done differently?

It is important to realise that the way we talk to others, has a strong influence on their feelings. Children especially are very sensitive to this. In the previous chapters, I demonstrated the link between communication, self-esteem and self-confidence in children. I also showed you how you can stimulate a growth mindset through your use of language.

The way you speak and your choice of words, together with your tone of voice (sincere, cheerful, uninterested), make all the difference in communication. Choose your words with care and try to focus on the positive side of things. If you only focus on what is not going well, you mainly confirm that this is indeed so, and you do not create the proper conditions for a pleasant and surprising reaction. Many people find it rather artificial to communicate differently than they are used to, but it is often the most important first step in improving various aspects of their lives. You do this by giving compliments and highlighting pleasant traits or behaviour that you appreciate and smiling. All these small signals contribute to a positive spiral interaction. A beautiful quote in this regard is the following:

*"Those who command the right word, offend no one.*
*Still, they tell the truth, their words are clear,*
*But never violent ... They will never*
*Be offended, and they will never offend anyone"*

*~ Buddha*

# Chapter 10: Augment Your Communication Skills

The framework offered by Thomas Gordon in regards to communication skills has always been a great help to me. This American psychologist became famous for the 'Gordon-method'. He introduced concepts such as 'active listening' the 'I message' and 'effective confrontations.'

In 1970 he wrote a bestselling book called 'Listening to children', in which he explains how educators and children can communicate more effectively, without adults abusing their power.

The Gordon method is based on the conviction that the use of power within relationships is harmful to relationships. Children who frequently lose battles because parents or educators use their power over them will often show the following behaviour or emotions:

- ✓ Resistance, rebellious, negativity

- ✓ Hatred, anger, animosity

- ✓ Aggression, vengefulness, retaliation

- ✓ Lies, concealment of feelings

- ✓ Blaming others, tell-tale behaviour, deceitful behaviour

- ✓ Dominating, tyrannical

- ✓ Absolutely wanting to win, not being able to handle losing very well

- ✓ Forming a pact, plotting against the parents

- ✓ Submission, obedience, accommodating behaviour, social desirability

- ✓ Wanting to curry favour

- ✓ Accommodating, lack of initiative, afraid of trying out something new

- ✓ Withdrawal, evasive, fantasising, regression

We have not even mentioned the myriad of physical complaints, such as stomach- and headaches. In short, these will not become, pleasant, social and responsible children. They will certainly not develop a growth mindset, nor a positive self-image.

Gordon regularly received parents who had problems raising their children. They told him that it had to do with their own upbringing and with the relationship that they had with their parents. Thomas Gordon felt for his clients. "Parents get the blame, but they do not receive help." This is why he started his very first parent course in Pasadena, California in 1962 called 'The Parent Effectiveness Training' (PET).

Many self-help books followed after this, which expanded his self-developed method in great detail. His approach stems from the willingness of parents to admit to prior mistakes and to learn from them. The desire to converge – which always begins with listening - restores genuine mutual respect between parents and children. His method translates these principles into a few concrete skills, which can be acquired through training and practice. The Gordon-skills, such as active listening and effective confrontation, can be applied everywhere and always.

A good relationship with your children, based on contact, bonding and fun, is what every parent wants, and yet parents can feel frustrated and powerless at times because of their children's behaviour. Young children do not wish to eat their dinner or go to bed. Or they spend hours on their computer. Older children often fight with their parents about the time that they have to be home, which more often than not leads to intense arguments. Parents frequently offer some reward or threaten with punishment thereby forcing their child to show 'desired' behaviour. Up to the point where this does not work anymore. Other parents are so indulgent that they become the losing party at one point.

The relationship between parent and child is perhaps the most important relationship in life. Children learn how to interact with others, by how their parents interact with them. All parents have certain expectations of their children and the relationship they build with them. A positive reaction contributes to the self-confidence of both parents and children and leads to a healthy development in children.

The starting point must be that every parent desires a healthy and loving relationship with their children. Good relationships are win-win relationships, which is to say, that there aren't any winners or losers in a positive relationship, the base of which is equality.

## *The language of acceptance*

One absolute condition for nurturing positive and loving communication is by accepting the other person unconditionally. When someone is capable of accepting the other 'as is', and is also able to show this or express it, he has the capacity to help the other.

The fact that he accepts the other the way they are is important in maintaining a relationship in which the other can grow and develop and learn to solve problems.

The language of acceptance gives the child the opportunity to express himself as well as to have the freedom to share his feelings and challenges with someone. The most important thing which can be achieved by showing acceptance is that deep inside the child will feel that you love him.

*Non-verbal transferal of acceptance:*

A smile, a wink, a pat on the back.

*Non-verbal transferal of non-acceptance:*

A frowning of the brows, a clicking of the tongue, looking away from someone.

An imperative thing to realise is that to start communicating in an open and positive way, you need to be able to accept yourself unconditionally. Which brings us back to the beginning of this book: Keep working on yourself and on your self-esteem! Invest primarily in the relationship with yourself. Your communication skills will definitely benefit from this as well.

## *Being clear*

Children have a great need for clarity. Comments such as, 'you are bad' or 'you are acting clumsy again', are very unclear messages for children. They feel the disapproval, but do not fully realise what is expected of them. Positive messages can also be unclear. 'You are sweet' is probably nicer to hear, but what does it really mean? This is why it is important to speak as clearly as possible. You can do this by saying what you think or feel, using 'I-messages'.

For example; 'I think you are sweet' is better than saying 'you are sweet'. You are even more specific when you point out the behaviour that you are happy about using 'I-messages'. For example: 'I think it is very sweet of you, for helping me out here' or, 'I'm very proud of you for tying your shoelaces, by yourself' or, 'It makes me feel very sad when I see you hit your sister.'

The Gordon method is based on equality in relationships, thereby allowing everyone to be themselves and take responsibility while taking the other into account. In parenting relationships, this translates into the educator showing the child respect and leaving the child in its worth. Actually, it is the democratic principles that are introduced within the family. The system emphasises effective communication and a solution based conflict resolution. The win-win principle is essential.

The Thomas Gordon parent training assumes that the parent is important, that the child is important, and that the relationship between the parent and child is important. This is why the ideal form of communication takes all three components into account. He proposes a six-step consultation method. The success of Thomas Gordon follows primarily from his ability to translate the educational theory in a concrete and practical form.

I was introduced to the Gordon method in one of my first jobs at an education counselling service. It was a real eye-opener for me, and it was indeed the practical usefulness which prompted me to apply the method to my own life. The first phase was working on the relationship I had with my husband. I practised the skills that Gordon offered and quickly noticed how well this worked. Our relationship grew stronger because the method challenges you to actually listen to the underlying motives of the other. At the same time, it challenges you to communicate in a much more precise way and to reflect on your true intentions and feelings in your communication with others.

## *Active listening*

It is a funny thing to realise that we spend years of our lives, from day-care to school, learning how to speak, to read and to write. But what about listening? Have you been taught how to listen to others to be able to truly understand the other? Probably not.

We are often poised to, being understood; we wish to make our point clear to the other. Due to this form of communication we often completely neglect the other. We pretend to listen, but we are only focused on a selection of the conversational items on the table. And those are the ones that you can use again in your reactions. You interpret everything that the other states from your own personal frame of reference and then you frequently conclude what the other is going to say, even before he has finished speaking. Does that sound familiar? We then say things like, "I know exactly what you mean!" or "Oh, I had the same thing the other day!" or "Do you know what I always do in a situation like that?"

This is all very understandable and I am also a master at filling in the words for the other person (ask my husband!). However due to Thomas Gordon and his training methods I have undertaken, I have become much more aware of this and subsequently try to shift to listening mode. If you actually listen and keep silent, you open yourself completely for the other person's story. You encourage the other person to speak freely and comprehensively until finished.

Active listening goes one step further. Active listening is about making a connection on an emotional level. It hands us a way to listen that is especially well suited to a situation in which the other wants to share a problem with you.

Mind you, Thomas Gordon does not offer any techniques and instruments that you can use at random. It starts with a basic attitude from which to engage your conversation with the other and build a relationship.

A good and effective listening attitude begins with the assumption of equality, of mutual respect and the willingness to invest in the other person. Otherwise, these are empty techniques which will not have the desired effect.

Active listening has the power to produce changes in mutual relationships and in the life and behaviour of other people. It leads to a more open and less defensive way of communication, and it creates much more harmony and emotional involvement.

It is about really giving the other the feeling that you actually hear and see, him or her, in the emotion of the Moment and active listening is about recognising underlying feelings.

Active listening can help children during their education to voice their opinions when they experience problems. As a parent, you need to use your inner radar to scan your child's feelings to determine what is bothering the child. However, as stated before, it is not a trick, it is a base attitude:

1. It is important that you truly wish to hear what your child wants to say.

2. You must really want to help your child with the problem the problem that he or she faces at that moment.

3. You must be able to accept your child's feelings completely.

4. You must have an ironclad confidence that your child can handle and process his or her feelings and is able to find solutions for his or her problems.

5. Do not forget that feeling's are of a temporary nature. (feelings change)

6. Try to see your child as a separate individual; every child is unique, and certainly not an extension of yourself or your partner.

When someone trusts us with their problems, we are more often than not inclined to force the other person to look at the problem differently or to offer solutions. This reaction usually stems from our own perception, our own experiences or our own ability on how to handle the problem which the other person is telling us. This stops us from actually listening to the other in such a way that the other person really feels understood. It is precisely this way of listening which can help the other person, organise his own thoughts and maybe even name a possible solution for himself. This works for adults as well as children in the same way.

## What is active listening?

Active listening requires us to be sensitive to the feelings of the other, from the perspective of what the other is communicating to us. Active listening desires clearly, from the receiver that he puts his own thoughts and feelings aside to be able to give complete attention to what is being said. You are forced to stand and listen carefully. If you are open to the experience of the other, it may well be possible that you will have to revise your own experiences about similar situations in the past. Your reaction will then not only reflect the actual words that have been said but the total message as well. You react to the underlying feeling that the other gives you. Do not say: 'Clean up your toys now, because we are going to eat', but 'I see that you are still having fun playing. Will you come and eat shortly?' Do not say 'Do not touch that', but: 'I understand that you would love to play with that, but this is really too dangerous for you, and that is why I am putting it away now.'

## Active listening is about the total message

Every message that someone wants to put forward has two components: The content and the underlying emotion or interpretation. With active listening, you take both levels into the communication. If children see that you take them into account too, the will feel that they are being taken seriously, and they will be sooner inclined to listen to you.

An example:

*Imagine you are cleaning your seven-year-old daughter's room and you have asked her to help you. You keep giving her a new task, as soon as she has finished the previous one. Imagine that she has started to collect all her socks in a basket. After a few minutes, she says: "I am done with the socks" while sighing deeply. You can choose to give her the next assignment immediately. But do you believe that she will start enthusiastically, that she feels as if she is seen and that there is a connectedness with you, while together you continue cleaning up?*

*Now picture an entirely different reaction, such as 'That was quite hard, wasn't it?' or 'That were a lot of socks, I am so glad that you have helped me with that'. Something that lets her know that you react to the fact she has let you know that she did not like this chore at all. Do you feel the difference in your reaction? And can you imagine the difference in the way that she will move on to her next chore? That is the power of active listening.*

## Why do parents wish to learn to listen actively?

- ✓ Active listening has some form of healing effect, it helps your children to discover exactly what it is that they are feeling.

- ✓ Active listening helps children to be less afraid of negative feelings.

- ✓ Active listening promotes a warm relationship between parents and child. The experience that you are being heard and understood by the other gives so much satisfaction that the transmitter feels affection about the listener. If you put yourself completely into the shoes of the other person, you will feel involvement and love.

✓ Active listening makes it easier for the child to solve his problems. If people can discuss a problem, it will lead to better results than when they only think about it.

✓ Active listening gives the child a chance. When parents react to their children's problems by actively listening, they will notice that the children will often start to think for themselves.

✓ Active listening causes the child to think for himself, to seek self-diagnosis for his problem and to discover his own solutions.

✓ By actively listening, a child is prompted to be more open to the thoughts and feelings of parents. Children will be more receptive to their parent's messages if their parents are willing to hear them out first.

Active listening demands quite a bit from you and is not something you can do all day. Active listening is especially useful in those situations where the other person needs your help, not by instantly providing a solution, but especially in those cases, active listening can provide exactly what the other needs. The feeling that, it is not strange what is going on inside of him or her and from that point on, search for a way to handle the situation.

# *Effective confrontations*

What I notice each and every time is, that when I take good care of myself and I listen to my own needs, my communication skills are at their best. When I am tired, emotional or stressed out, it is much harder for me to communicate in an open and loving way with my family. I often put myself in the victim role, I accuse everyone wrongfully, and I catch myself making manipulative statements.

That is why I always emphasise why it is so important for parents to take good care of themselves. It means that they cannot disregard themselves, that they must know their own needs, that they must pay attention to their requirements, and that they ensure that their own cup is full. Gordon calls this the filled cup theory. It is important that your own cup is full. Otherwise, you will not have anything to share or to give to the other.

This can mean something different for every parent; sleep is vital for one, while the other finds a regular night out on the town important. The cup can be filled in various ways.

# *Establishing limits*

If you wish to stand up for your own needs, you cannot do so without setting limits; limits to your own willingness to comply with requests from others and limits to what you consider being the unacceptable behaviour of others.

If your colleague asks you to take over a job of her but you are busy, then it is important to send out a clear no: No, I do not have time for that, right now.

If your child asks you to read a book and you are just reading a book yourself, then you can say: No, I do not want to read it now because I am just reading a book myself.

Having difficulty with establishing limits often has to do with fear of damaging the relationship. Gordon offers us other ways to set your own limits effectively.

It is important to realise, that each parent has other limits. So, while a father may find it perfectly acceptable that his 3-year-old son eats without cutlery, Mum may find it completely unacceptable. Whether you accept your child's behaviour or not also depends on how you look at your child's behaviour at that moment. This may vary per situation and per child. While at one moment, you may find throwing water unacceptable, on a hot tropical day you might not object to it. You may accept a 2-year-old child not to put his toys away after playing but you will expect it from your 12-year-old child.

The parenting myth of "always being consistent" is thus brought down. I found it a great relief to learn because consistency is not always convenient. It puts enormous pressure on us, to always want to be consistent and it gets even more complicated when Mum and Dad always want to be on the same page. Mum and Dad are in fact different people with different limits. We do not need to be 100% consistent. If we communicate effectively and clearly, we can express why we allow certain behaviour now, and not at another time, or why we accept the conduct of a smaller brother, but not from his big sister. Or why something is not allowed by Mum but is okay with grandma.

For example. Grandma allows certain behaviour because grandmothers love spoiling their grandchildren. This is what grandmothers are for. Even though Mum does not approve because Mum wants to teach you … (Fill in the blank).

It is good to take a pause for a minute here and explore whether your limits are needed at all. We frequently prohibit our children from doing all sorts of things, because we think this is how it should be. Maybe because we were not allowed ourselves or because we believe that it is expected socially. When my first daughter started her 'why-phase', around the age of two, I felt significantly challenged. She asked me 'why' about everything, and for me, it was not always easy to answer her questions!

Why does your child always have to eat her entire sandwich? Why should your child not be allowed to run? Why does he need to be in bed by 7 o'clock? If you can explain it well, then that is fine, but sometimes I could not.

My daughter, Amber, always felt hot, which is why she always refused to put on her coat. Even in winter when she went outside to play. "Amber put your coat on!" "But why?" "Otherwise, you will get cold". "But I'm warm!" Indeed she would have rosy cheeks from the warmth, and she was never ill.

I decided to give up the 'coat' battle, even though other mothers came by to tell me that my little girl was playing outside with no coat on. When I replied that I was aware of this, they were very puzzled, but if you cannot explain why you allow things, then what kind of rule is it?

Alright, back to establishing limits – as sometimes something is just not allowed which you can explain, even though we often do not. Children need loving limitations and Gordon teaches us to establish limits in a positive and effective manner.

It is of particular importance, to be honest about your thoughts and feelings. Nothing is more unclear for a child than non-verbally emanating disapproval, without voicing it. Gordon calls this pretence acceptance. If your posture, on the other hand, reflects what you say, then you are open and honest, and the child will understand what it is that you mean.

Use the three-part I-message. If your child does something that you do not accept, it will be optimally effective if you confront him with an I-message that consists of three parts. You call on:

- ✓ The behaviour of the child

- ✓ Your own feelings

- ✓ The consequences that the behaviour has for you.

## How does this work in practice?

For example, your eleven-year-old daughter does not come home on time. You had agreed to go shopping together, but there is no time left for that, and you are worried as well.

## Your child's behaviour

It is important to describe negative behaviour as clearly as possible, without judgement.

So in this case: Your child is not home on time.

## Your own feeling

Share how your feel about this and why.

So in this case: You are worried as well as irritated because you have not had the time to go shopping.

## Result of the behaviour for you as a parent

Name the consequence of this behaviour.

So in this case: the consequence is the unpleasant feeling of concern and not being able to go shopping together.

In this case, the complete three-part I-message will be:

"You were not at home at 4 o'clock, as we had agreed. I was worried about you. Besides, it is now too late to go shopping, and I was really looking forward to that."

Many parents that I have trained over the last years feel resistance at first with this way of establishing limits. They believe that it sounds unnatural and fake. Or they indicate that they do not have the time to have to explain everything in this way, the whole day. Or they believe that this will not work with their children. What kind of resistance do you feel?

I felt the same way, and sometimes I simply did not feel like doing it at all! Do not do anything that does not suit you and find a way in how you wish to deal with your children that you feel comfortable with. Look for your own wordings, so that it feels like you. My experience is that this way of communication requires practice. It can challenge you enormously, yet it yields a great deal and is, therefore, effective.

The benefit of I-messages is that they respect the child so that they do not feel judged. This produces less resistance with the child than with the you-messages (why are you late again? I can never count on you!), and the child is much more willing to listen. Besides this, the child receives the responsibility to help find a solution, and that encourages his independence. Your child really wants you to be happy, and if you indicate from within yourself that something is bothering you, then most children will be willing to help and think about possible solutions.

Three part I-messages are often too complicated for very young children. It is often clearer for them if that which you say is followed with action. If your one-year-old son kicks you while on your arm, you can put him on the ground while saying: "It hurts me when you kick me".

Offering an alternative for the unacceptable behaviour can also help: Your two-year-old daughter wants to draw on the wall with crayons, you hand her a large sheet of paper while saying: "Draw on this, I think it is a shame to mark a clean wall by you drawing on it".

By communicating in an open, honest and transparent manner, you can stand up for your own needs as a parent and avoid conflicts that cost time and energy. By communicating clearly, you are filling your cup. You are also offering a good example to your child. Your child will learn to have consideration with you and with others as well as how to voice his own needs. Holding your own ground while taking the other into account is what you live for.

## *The seven characteristics of effective families*

Another inspiration for me is Stephen Covey. In his book "The Seven Habits of Highly Effective People" Covey describes how you can be happier and more effective in life and how you can be more effective as a leader of people. The book is the result of extensive research into the principles of success. Covey argues that long-term and continuous success is only possible if you live according to principal values. He encapsulates these principle values into seven universal characteristics. This book has been on the managers' bestsellers list for years now.

According to Covey, his principles are also true for family life. People often indicate that family is very important and that they would give up everything for them. But if you ask to look closely at the lifestyle of the family members, and look at what it is that they pay the most attention to, then it is often either work, friends and hobbies. People find it difficult to fulfil what they deem to be important. Yet family members have a long-lasting influence on each other and each other's development. In his book "The Seven Habits of Highly Effective Families" he translates his insights to family life.

This book is geared at the creation of an optimal family culture. It delves deeper, among other things, into the question of how to best handle differences within your family, how to put yourself into the other persons' shoes to form a better whole as a family. Covey addresses the seven characteristics for the creation of an effective and optimal family relationship.

**Try to understand first and to be understood later**

This is the fifth aspect that Covey describes in his book. Most conversations that people have on a daily basis are simple conversations. They conduct some sort of monologue with each other, whereas we all could be listening with more empathy. When you do this, you place yourself in the world of thought of the other person, and you will be able to achieve more. When you listen with empathy, you can try to use your influence, and try to make things clearer and perhaps even effect change.

He distinguishes 3 phases for empathic listening:

- ✓ Try to repeat the content of the other person

- ✓ Try to summarise the content in your own words

- ✓ Show your feeling

Understanding first is the first step to a win-win situation. We can clearly see a parallel with the 'active listening' from the Gordon-method. Being understood yourself is a logical consequence, according to Covey.

We communicate a great deal in our family. Thanks to Covey we have been planning - ever since the youngest was two years old – every year during the Christmas holidays, a moment to reflect, as a family, on the year which is nearly over, and we set goals for the year to come. It has become a tradition that I have come to cherish.

Now that the children have grown older, they have gained a larger and more active input in the matter, but even when they were smaller they were involved and loved participating. Sometimes you are really flabbergasted at the wisdom and the attentiveness that young children have within them. Never underestimate them!

When the children were younger, I wrote a monthly column, the 'Digidaal' for my consultancy firm, at the time, 'Daaladvies'. In one of my first columns from 2007, (my children were ages, 9, 5, 3 and 1). I wrote about club meetings that were held regularly at our house. I wrote this:

*"Every so often a child's voice shouts Club meeting, in a loud and attention seeking tone of voice. Our four children will then appear out of every nook and cranny of the house and will run together, to a 'secret' or in any case 'own' place, preferably the treehouse or the big sister's room, where all manner of exciting attributes can be found. The door will then slam shut and be locked, Club meeting.*

*Important matters are discussed, planned and prepared during these club meetings, such as new games complete with matching rules, to devious plans and surprises for Mum and Dad. Funny how children at this early age realise that it is necessary to get together from time to time and boost the old team spirit. Even though they can be at each other's throats at times, because the individual interests do not always match, they do realise that they have to do it together and that it is necessary to keep everyone on the same page."*

Next to the family mission we began to hold a weekly family meeting. At our house, this takes place every Sunday morning, after breakfast. And guess what? Our youngest, who is nine years old is very often the chairman! He prepares the agenda items, summarises the meeting and keeps order (and that is necessary at times too). Sometimes it is a light-hearted conversation, and sometimes harsher words are used and feelings, of which we had not been aware of, are shared too.

Over the years we have adapted the form of these meetings to the ages of the children. We usually discuss the following items: What is on everyone's mind? How is everybody? Are there any organisational or domestic issues that need to be addressed? And every so often we add a theme to the mix. Sometimes we talk about an artist, a newsworthy event, or emotion. Sometimes someone has something that he or she has researched and wants to share with the rest of the family.

Of course, not everyone feels like participating in a family meeting, and especially the adolescents protest from time to time. Do we really have to do this? But in the end, even they see the value of these conversations. We get to know each other much better and along the way we have all learned how to express our feelings to one another, and to make things negotiable. That has certainly strengthened our team spirit.

Believe me, it is not always as peaceful and harmonious as we would like, but without friction, there is no fire! I am convinced that by creating these family moments, the six of us have become a strong team. A team that dares to chase dreams and realise them too.

## *Non-violent communication*

Marshall Rosenberg, a psychologist and communication trainer, states that the way we often communicate - unintentionally - is more violent than we realise. We use expressions which are often unnecessarily accusatory. Nobody wants that. To avoid this, he developed the concept of "Nonviolent Communication".

In this communication connection is central: Relationship with oneself, with others and with life. In the Dutch language the term 'connective communication' is increasingly used instead of 'non-violent communication'.

In this connection, there is room for clarity and compassion. You connect to what actually lives inside of you and the other person; you communicate your feelings and the underlying needs. You take full responsibility for them. This in contrast to judging, condemning and blaming, which we all know so well and have come to consider as being normal. In this way we can get in touch with each other on a different level than being right or wrong, particularly that of the belly and the heart. You communicate with your head, your stomach and your heart (and soul).

To take people through the thought steps of non-violent communication, Rosenberg uses two hand puppets: A jackal and a giraffe.

The Jackal symbolises the violent, space creating communication. The jackal, like the wolf and the coyote, belongs to the dog-like predators. The jackal is rather small, is low on the ground and has narrow tunnel vision.

The giraffe symbolises the nonviolent, connective communication. The giraffe looks at everything and has a broad view (helicopter view). Because the giraffe is tall, she can hear and feel much better and take in what she sees ...

Rosenberg writes the following:

*"Force a child to obey you and you will sooner or later pay the price. If you would really like someone else to do something, there are two questions you should ask yourself in advance. First: What you want the other to do? And: What are their reasons to be able to comply with your request? In other words, you want someone to do something on their own accord and not because of some illegitimate obedience."*

## *Practice makes perfect*

In the books of Gordon, Covey and Marshal many case examples are given. They hand us exercises and linguistic aids to increase our awareness of positive and loving communication. Perhaps some phrases and examples can sound a bit artificial. This is something I also heard from many parents when I was still giving communication training. It does not feel 'real'. That is also true in the beginning because your way of communicating is so deeply ingrained and frequently the result of how you were raised, and the way your parents communicated with you, as a child.

However, experience shows that being aware of our use of language - and the underlying ideas - is achieved the easiest, by sticking to our intention and by calmly practising, even if it does not work right away. Children will also not react immediately in the desired manner, only because it does not feel natural to you yet and because you have already built a particular pattern together from birth. Give yourself and your children time to get used to a new way of communicating and time to strengthen the mutual trust.

If we want to change our way of communication in our daily lives, it is important to keep in mind that it is something other than a set of rules. It is a process that develops, depending on the situation, on personal and cultural styles and on our own capacity for compassion and empathy. Keep the message that you pass along pure and exclusively to yourself, and accept that a positive, loving communication is an art form, that arises only after some practice, for most of us.

## *Soul Talk*

I agree with Marshal Gordon and Covey that communication is not just about the use of certain techniques and strategies. The most powerful communication is the communication from the heart. At the moment I am reading the book Living Big by Pam Grout, and I really liked reading about an expression from Northern Russia, which translates to 'Soul Talk' in English. In Russia it means something like 'speaking from the heart, speaking of the great things in life'. Grandparents, children and grandchildren sit together under the old oak tree and talk to each other about the things that matter to them. These discussions have been known to go on for hours.

Although our conversations do not last for hours, I find the term Soul Talk charming, and in our weekly family meetings, I frequently experience how valuable the things are that we share with each other. Like last Sunday, when my oldest son told us that since the death of our cat - right before our immigration - he often felt scared. He suddenly realised that you can just die like that, or - even scarier - Mum and Dad could - a feeling that we all recognise.

How sad is it that, according to a study I read once in the New York Times, the average parent in America only spends 10 minutes a day conversing with his child? Even the stay-at-home Mums scored just a bit over 15 minutes.

Let us make some more time available to talk to our children about big things, about our big dreams and our great fears. Your children need to hear what you think, to know who you are. Then afterwards they can reflect on who they are and learn that a big idea is much more significant than a big car.

## Important lessons and insights from Part 5

### For yourself

- ✓ Communication is an essential ability in people's lives. Relationship = Communication.

- ✓ An absolute condition for a positive and loving communication is accepting the other completely for who he or she is.

- ✓ Unconditional acceptance of yourself is necessary to be able to truly achieve this.

- ✓ Gordon, Covey and Marshall offer meaningful frameworks to help you improve your own communication skills.

### In relation to your child(ren)

- ✓ The way you communicate with your child is of the utmost importance for the development of his or her self-image and self-esteem

- ✓ The relationship between parent and child is perhaps the most important relationship in life. The way parents handle their child, teaches them how they will interact with others.

- ✓ Investing in a positive family communication and formulating a family mission is fun to do and offers a sustainable investment in the common relationships within the family.

In Part 5 we contemplated, loving communication. The e-Book 'Loving communication with your child' contains a myriad of practical tips for everyday situations.

To gain access to this loving gift, go to: www.nolimitparenting.com/bonuses or scan this QR-code.

# *Part 6*

## Make the COMMITMENT to keep on track (keep moving)

*You need to make a commitment, and once you make it,*
*Then life will give you some answers.*

*~ Les Brown*

# Trust Yourself, Others, and Life and Pass This Trust on to Your Children

In this final chapter, I will discuss the realisation of your dreams. When you learn to let go of trust and you switch from willpower to inspired action, you will find that your life will flow without exertion. By living fully and limitless, you give your children the freedom to do the same. I want to help you on your way to actually get into action and hold the focus if you really want to change your life.

You started out in Part 1, working on your self-esteem and on loving yourself, which is the basis of happiness and satisfaction. Then we touched on the subject of making choices from the heart and from your personal values. In Part 3 you were introduced to mindfulness, mindful living and enjoyment. Focusing on the present, and on the things that are vital to you and seeking to squelch your opinion and your judgements a bit more.

From this peace of mind, you went in search of your passion in Part 4. What are you good at, what lights your fire? In Part 5 we examined your way of communicating. Communication is a tool for maintaining relationships with people who are important to you. Now, the time has come to integrate all of these parts and to determine a clear vision for your life and to come into action to effectively realise this vision. That is available for everyone, including you and your children!

Realise that if you want to change something in your life, you will need to change yourself first. You probably know the phrase: "If you do what you always did, you will get what you always got."

So if you want to ask something else from life, then ask yourself what change you have to make:

- ✓ From floating (idea, dream, concept, spirituality) to feet on the ground (result, success, product, material).

- ✓ From goals (head, effort) to feeling (heart, relaxation)

- ✓ From workaholic to 'inspired action.'

- ✓ From procrastination to a 'start-before-you-ready'-mentality.

You know best what applies to you. It must become your passion for achieving your own goals and creating your own perfect life!

As a first step, 'Formulating your dream life' may sound quite grand and strange for some people, and it can scare them off. I often did this exercise during training sessions and asked: "If nothing could hold you back and if money were not an issue and if the past had no influence on the future … what would you wish for yourself? For your life?"

Some people just shut down or became emotional as a result of this question. If this is the case with you, be aware of the thoughts and the feelings that arise within you.

- ✓ Do I really deserve that?

- ✓ But then I will have to work really hard or change!

- ✓ That is not meant for me, right?

- ✓ Well, a little bit better is also good, I do not need a dream life, right away.

- ✓ But that is not me, I am not good enough.

These are your blockages that hinder you to live the life that you actually want to live. Check and see if you can discover where these convictions come from. I have wondered if that multicultural girl, born and raised in a high-rise apartment in Rotterdam-South in the Netherlands, should have so much pretence, and still, I had my dreams. That I would rise above my parent's income level, that I would have a large family, and that I would go to university. But not in my wildest dreams could I have imagined that my life would unfold as it has done in the past twenty years. I could never have imagined that my future would look so bright.

I look at my life with intense gratitude and amazement. Amazement about the magical working of the universe and appreciation for the continuing expansion of my consciousness, which has brought me a new phase in my life during the past year. Before I delve deeper into the question of how to realise your dream life, I would like to share my personal story with you about the manifestation of our dream.

As of late 2012, we decided that it was time for a new adventure. We had been living in Curaçao, a magnificent island in the Caribbean, since 2009, where we spent six wonderful years. But all six of us felt that it was time for something new. Curaçao had become too small for us and had little to offer a family with four growing children. So, we held many family meetings.

Moving back to the Netherlands was not an option (yet) for any of us. We could always do that. We decided to examine our wishes. Beautiful nature, good schooling, a stable democracy and economy, English speaking, great weather, urban, culture, nice shops with a varied selection products, good food, and sports facilities. All family members offered their input, and we decided on Australia. First Melbourne, but because of the climate, we soon decided on Sydney.

We did not know then that it would take us two and a half years before we could actually move to Australia, but you cannot come to Australia, just like that.

We spent two and a half years searching for an immigration agent. Then we had to take endless English proficiency tests in Miami (because international tests could not be taken in Curaçao). Official documents had to be translated into English by a certified translator, which then had to be authenticated by an authorised notary. We had to produce financial statements to prove that we were economically viable and request letters of reference from previous employers (up to ten years back!) as well as apply for certificates of good behaviour and a medical examination of all six family members, which consisted of blood tests to lung x-rays.

We did it all, step by step, without knowing where this story was going to end and whether we would ever get our coveted visas. During this time the regulations often changed or it turned out that other requirements were demanded than those that we thought were required at an earlier stage.

And during this period our lives went on as usual. But all of our choices were influenced by our shared dream, whether we realised it or not. Whether or not to buy a new car, whether or not to transfer the children to English-language education, whether or not to go on holidays, and so on. For us, as adults, it was difficult enough to lead such a double life, let alone for the children.

Many times the answer of my heroine, Louise Hay passed through my head. To the question on how she had managed to build her million dollar company, Hay House Publishers, Louise invariably replies: "I picked up my phone and answered my email." With this, she indicates that every time, you just take the step that presents itself, an important key in manifesting your dreams.

Later on, I will mention some other important keys for creating changes in your life. But in essence, it all comes down to this: Expand your consciousness. Know that there is always more possible than you can imagine.

Regarding our dream. On June 15, 2015, the big day finally arrived. Around midnight we received the liberating email from our immigration agent that we had received the coveted Permanent Resident Visa! Now I know that everything presents itself in our lives at just the right time. All the information, all the money, all the strength you need is already there. If you had told me ten years ago that I would immigrate to Australia in 2015, I would most likely not have believed you. Something like that would have never have occurred to me. I discovered that taking the step to move to Curacao from the Netherlands was a big enough deal already. At the time I would not have thought that I would be ready for another big move.

This awareness makes me so happy because it shows how we are able to expand our consciousness. Something that does not arise in your consciousness at this moment may well do so at a later time. A beautiful and fulfilling life is within reach for all of us. You just have to imagine it.

If you are willing to work on loving yourself and trusting life. If you are ready to work on your blockades and face your fears, as well as daring to follow your heart – regardless of what other people think – then true happiness is waiting for you and the universe will reward your courage. Are you ready for this?

# Chapter 11: Take Responsibility for Your Own Life But Not For That of Others

Many people, especially women and oldest children, feel responsible for too many things. These people believe that they need to help everyone around them and solve their problems. As parents, we really want to address our children's problems. In our relationships, we wish to solve our partner's problems and as employees those of our boss. This might seem to be a very noble and positive thing, but this exaggerated helpfulness has another side. By trying to solve other people's problems, you take away the opportunity for them to solve their own problems. More importantly, you deprive the other person of that wonderful feeling you get when you actually solve or overcome a difficult situation yourself. You were dreading something, but you did it anyway! You ran into a problem, but you came up with a solution all by yourself! Wow, that really gives you a feeling of accomplishment.

Another disadvantage of this self-imposed feeling of responsibility is that it is hard for yourself. If you spend all day not only being concerned about your own problems and responsibilities, but also wanting to solve other people's problems, you burden yourself enormously. You do not need to carry the weight of the world on your shoulders!

There is no escaping the fact that this pressure of problem solving will overwhelm you at some point. This can manifest itself through physical symptoms (such as a headache or tension in your neck and shoulders), but also in gloom or an unexpected and unnecessary explosion of rage. Sometimes it stays smouldering under the surface, but you become irritable or cranky.

The opposite also happens. We lay blame elsewhere. We either blame others or the system, the organisation. This can also deplete us. It is nothing more than a defence mechanism. By always pointing your finger, you do not have to look at yourself. We think it is too difficult, too confrontational or too painful. We do not look inward. But this victim role will break us in the long term. It takes you away from your own strength. You become tired and lose pleasure in the things you do.

Take full responsibility for your own feelings, needs, actions and life, and leave those of others where they rightfully belong, with the other! That is the only way you will manage to change your life in a direction that you want.

# Chapter 12: 'Address What's Bugging You'

When my youngest child was having a difficult period at school and it even appeared likely that he was going to become a victim of bullying I read 'Goodbye, Bumps' to him, endlessly. The book was written by Wayne Dyer, and was co-written by his youngest daughter Saje Dyer. In this book, children learn that when you experience something unpleasant, you can change your attitude on it, and not allow it to gain power over you. A valuable lesson.

In the story, Saje tells of a period in her life - she was five years old at the time - in which was tormented by red bumps on her face. The doctor did not know what it was and suggested to just wait and see if they would go away. Saje found the waiting hard and her father proposed to talk to the bumps. He said, "Hi pimples, I do not know exactly why you are here, but I'm ready to let you go. Thank you for your presence, but I will let you go now." After a week of these conversations, the pimples disappeared.

One way of making peace with whatever it is that is bothering you is to understand that it is there for a reason and to consciously declare that you want to let it go. Through this change in attitude, you will notice that what had bothered you so much is not as bad as you might have thought, after all. By not giving the problem your devoted attention, it will affect you much less.

You cannot change everything that happens to you, but you can always change your attitude toward what happens to you. Let the negative feelings that you have about certain situations go and make it less important in your life. Know that you will feel happier and freer, when you consciously choose to let go of these feelings. Not out of anger or helplessness, but with the full knowledge and acceptance of the situation or what is happening. Whether it be: Having big ears, not having enough money, weight issues, freckles, a scar, a partner who is not 'perfect', an annoying boss or poor eyesight. Everything will be placed in a different light when you change your attitude towards it.

# Chapter 13: Dare to Dream, Make Contact with Your Deepest Desires

Make contact with your deepest desire, your personal mission. Imagine the end result and keep this in mind. Dream big. Truly believe that your dreams will come true. Of course there will be obstacles along the way, but just take action. Imagine every step along the way as a seed that you plant.

My husband and I felt that life held more in store for us. We want to live meaningful lives, we want to offer our children more possibilities, and show them the world and of the beauty of it. We want to experience more, to learn more, to enjoy and to grow more. We wish to expand our boundaries, to expand our consciousness. That is our mission, and that is my desire. What is yours?

Do not let impending thoughts and convictions sabotage your efforts to make contact with your dreams and desires. We sabotage ourselves by thinking things, such as:

- ✓ I do not have enough experience

- ✓ I am stuck with my mortgage

- ✓ I am too old or too young

- ✓ I cannot just turn my life upside down

- ✓ There is a crisis

- ✓ I cannot start again

- ✓ I cannot change

- ✓ This is my character

All of the above are ideas that are stuck in your head and you have no way of knowing, whether they are really true or not! Stop giving these thoughts any more attention or energy. Thank them for wanting to protect you. Know that you are not in danger. Believe in yourself and be prepared to make your dreams come true.

Building up to our emigration to Australia, I experienced what kind of force dreams can generate. By visualising them, as if they are already here, you put something in motion.

So, for the last three years on December 31 at 9:00 in the morning, we sat in front of the TV to watch the magnificent firework display at the Harbour Bridge in Sydney, the first city in the world where the New Year begins. And we imagined ourselves standing there.

For two and a half years we read the Sydney Morning Herald. We all had a screen saver on our mobile phone, laptop or iPad, of Sydney, and we dreamt of all the beautiful places we wanted to visit there.

During two and a half years we immersed ourselves in Australia, we watched TV programmes of people who had emigrated there, and we pictured ourselves flying over on a Qantas plane and setting foot on Australian soil.

I personally imagined myself writing my blogs in English, how I would come into contact with peers and how my first book in English was going to be published. How my personal workspace would look over there, and the view that I would have there. How my children would discover Australian nature, how we would go on family camping trips and how they would thrive in the Australian educational system.

That was my goal, those were my dreams. There was no room for a plan B.

# Chapter 14: Forgive Yourself and Others

Forgiving yourself and others frees you from your past. If you find yourself stuck in life, I'm pretty sure there is something left to forgive. If your life does not flow, it usually means that you are holding on to something that happened in the past. It can be regret or feelings of sadness. Or maybe your feel scared or guilty or embarrassed by past issues. Maybe you are harbouring a feeling of resentment, or anger or vengefulness. All these feelings can hinder you if you do not want to forgive or if you refuse to let go. This frustrates you to live and unlock your future in the present moment, as it is intended.

We have all been hurt at one point or another. We were treated poorly, our trust was violated or perhaps our hearts were broken, and although this pain is normal, sometimes the pain will drag on a little longer. You relive the pain over and over, and you have difficulty letting go of it.

This causes problems. It not only makes you unhappy, but can also complicate or ruin relationships, distract you from your work, your family and other important things, and it can give you a closed personality, thus causing you to struggle to be open to new things and new people. You get caught up in a cycle of anger and pain, while the beauty of life passes you by.

It is important that we learn to let go, to forgive so that we are able to move on and be happy. Forgiveness does not mean erasing the past or forgetting what happened or that you approve of the other person's behaviour. It does not even mean the other person will change his behaviour; you have no power over that. It means that you are releasing the anger and pain your feel so that the other person no longer has any power over you. It is not easy. But you can learn how to do this. This is not something I say lightly. It was a lesson I also had to learn.

When I had forgiven my father, I managed to feel the love - that had been blocked for years - for him again. A great burden fell off me, and suddenly I was able to access the beautiful memories that were there too. No one is entirely bad or totally good. It is as simple as that. Above all, forgiveness is a gift to yourself. As you forgive the other person, you free yourself.

Sometimes you do not experience a sufficient "burden" to really change anything about it. Sometimes you are just not ready to let go of something, of someone or a situation. You are not ready for it because it provides some sort of benefit for you. There is a profit in your loss. If that profit is big and if it means that you have to get out of your comfort zone to change that situation, then it will not matter what you do, because it will not work. We talk of mixed neurological associations. Or simpler said: Mixed feelings. The impulses in your nervous system say: I want to turn left, but I also want to right. The result is that you will remain right where you are.

On the other hand, when you are ready to let go, and you make a firm decision to, for example, forgive yourself or the other (when you choose to give another meaning to what has happened in your life), you learn from what was so that you are able to make different choices from now on. Sometimes it is amazing how quickly and how easy it is to let go. Also and perhaps especially in those very extreme and painful situations in your life.

**The following tips can be of help to you:**

- ✓ Make the conscious choice to let go.

- ✓ Understand that you are responsible for your own happiness.

- ✓ Focus on the present and experience how it feels when your burden is no longer weighing you down.

- ✓ Allow peace in your life. Choose peace.

- ✓ Feel compassion. For the other person and for yourself.

- ✓ Do not force anything, allow time for the process.

# Chapter 15: Inspired Focus and Action Every Day

When you are on your way to achieving your dreams, always do that which presents itself. Follow the signals that you receive along the way. Focus, make choices and do not lose sight of your end goal, even for a minute. Do not persevere and endure purely on willpower and determination, but take the steps out of confidence and enthusiasm. Know that you are building a dream and that the process will unfold exactly in the way that is right for you.

Sometimes all the steps you need to take may seem overwhelming. You might think you will never achieve your final goal. When we were in the middle of our immigration process, sometimes we nearly lost all hope. But we kept focussing on that one step that we were taking at that time and let go of the steps we still needed to take to reach our goal.

We worked on ourselves with affirmations, we made mood boards, we held family meetings and shared our feelings, we looked at beautiful pictures of Sydney, or we joined Facebook groups of Dutch people living in Sydney as well as DutchLink. When you are pregnant, you suddenly see pregnant women everywhere. In our case, it was the same in regards to Australia. Time after time we kept meeting people who had been to Australia or had lived there and who confirmed that it was a great country and that we could live a great life over there.

Most importantly, we remained focused on our dream, our final goal. No plans B or C. First we wanted to go to complete plan A. With complete focus, and no room for anything else, because that would only distract us.

Taking action is often the best medicine for dealing with fear, doubt, uncertainty, and unrest. It will only go away by doing something! Take that next step, every time. The longer you postpone things that you find daunting, the more dramatic they become. Surround yourself with affirmations that help you maintain focus on your goals and your dreams. Surround yourself with people who will help you maintain the right 'vibe' and most of all, stay active!

# Chapter 16: Do not Let Your Fears Determine the Course of Your Life

Conquering fear is an enormous threshold to overcome. Fear keeps you away from success. Fear dims your light and that is such a waste. You can hide to avoid having to confront your fears or you can stick your head in the sand and pretend the fear does not exist. In the end, you will either stay small or appear to be successful on the outside, but feeling miserable on the inside. By really knowing what your fears are, feeling them intensely, you can reverse your fears into power - the power needed to take the steps. Do you find it scary to take action? Find out where that fear comes from. Feel every fear that comes into your mind, all the way down into the very fibre of your body. Then you will notice that the fear becomes lighter. And then you can convert these feelings into strength and do it anyway. Feel the fear and then do it anyway.

Those who want to free themselves from fear, need to leave behind the things they are familiar with and to open themselves up to that which is in front of him: they have to make the unknown, known.

If you look at your current life as a timeline, the past is behind you and the future in front of you. If I ask you what your future looks like, you will probably say, "I do not know". Most people have no clear vision for their lives. From childhood on, we learn many things about life. We are told to work hard, make sacrifices, accept our fate or situation and stop wasting time daydreaming. So many people stop dreaming, and that is such a pity because to reach your goals, it is of vital importance that you dream about your desires and what it is you want in your life and that you set a date or a time schedule on that. This helps you to get into action to reach your goals.

> *It all depends on what you believe!*

In this framework, it is crucial to know what the 'comfort zone' is. Your comfort zone is a metaphor for that area in your life that you know, and that you are comfortable with. That which you are used to doing. The area where you feel that you have everything under control. Whether it is a pleasant experience or not, it is familiar to you.

So 'getting stuck in a traffic jam', 'having a fight with your partner', 'being yelled at by your boss', 'watching television at night on the couch' are your comfort zones, if and when these are daily or regular occurrences in your life. Also 'catching up with friends' or 'being greeted at night when you come home' are part of your comfort zone. They are your habits, your daily routines. Your convictions, your behaviour, your knowledge, and abilities that you use in these situations. All are part of your comfort zone.

Just outside your comfort zone is your 'learning zone'. In developmental psychology, this is called the 'the zone of proximal development'. The Soviet psychologist Vygotsky developed this concept, and it represents the difference between what a child can do without help and what they can do with help. Vygotsky, together with other educational experts, believes that it should be the role of schooling to provide children with experiences that are located in their zone of proximal development, thereby encouraging and stimulating their individual learning abilities.

You enter this area when you go out to learn new things and expand your knowledge.

For example, if you pick up a new language, go travelling and visiting new countries, you seek out new experiences and points of view, or expand into a new market with your business, or explore a new culture and build friendships with new people. This is the area where you experiment, observe, compare, learn, enjoy, and grow. Some people, like myself, love this area dearly. They discover new perspectives and search this area, not only willingly but also frequently.

Other people find it terribly scary to move in their zone of proximal development. They continue to prefer their comfort zone because they think it is dangerous to leave this.

One step further from your comfort zone lies the "panic zone", the area where you do not have any experience and that can lead to outright panic. People who prefer to stay in their comfort zone, regard the panic zone as the area where truly dangerous things may happen. They want to stay far away from it, because 'what if things go wrong?"

But what if things go well?

I am convinced that this panic zone is precisely the area where magical things await. Things that you do not know, things that you cannot identify. Because you have not been there yet.

The zone of the big challenges. If you are moving over there, you will expand your comfort zone, and you will expand your consciousness. You will become more and more aware of all that is possible. You grow.

People often do not dare to enter this area because they are afraid of losing what they have or who they are. In that regard, Thom (my stillborn son) gave me an important gift. If I could survive his loss, I could survive anything.

And yes, if you leave your comfort zone, your life changes, yet you lose nothing. Exactly the opposite is true, you become more yourself, and you get more in return. Whether it is knowledge, experience, money or love. Who knows what awaits you in this magical zone?

There are two distinct emotions to be distinguished during this process, which at times seem to work against each other, "emotional tension" and "creative tension". The first wants to keep you in the comfort zone (fear), and the other wants to pull you out (motivation). To grow, it is important that you learn to deal with the emotional tension, the fears that arise when you are considering leaving your comfort zone.

It is important to face your fears: Your fear of failure, your fear of what others think or say about you, your fear of embarrassment, fear or to be ridiculed. These fears have to go win your desires: More time with your family, more income, more 'inner peace', more harmony, more travel, and more work on your passion, whatever that may be.

This is where we come full circle again. How do you overcome those fears? By working on self-love, on your self-esteem and on your self- confidence. Believe in yourself! When you take small steps outside of your comfort zone, you build up your self-confidence, you enjoy positive experiences, which give you just enough courage to take the next step. And where there is more love (for yourself in this case, or for life and for your passion), there is less room for fear.

From this place of confidence, you will naturally discover your vision for your life. You will get to know yourself better (who) and your goals become will become clearer (what). You develop the confidence that your goals are achievable. The more you grow, the more space you give to the creative tension that you experience, and the more you will discover your values and your mission. What purpose lies below your goals (why)? All you now need to do now is take action. It's time to leave your comfort zone and pursue your dream. That feels scary, vulnerable and risky. You will not always have an immediate answer or solution, but hey, you are human after all.

Congratulations, you are now moving in the direction of your dream. Look back at your comfort zone, do not forget the skills, knowledge and experience that you can take with you to achieve your dream life. Use everything you have to realise your dream.

# Chapter 17: Be Thankful and Find the Right Frequency

The calling upon and experience of gratitude is an indispensable element when you want to develop a positive mindset. Be grateful for what already is, be thankful for your current situation.

This can be difficult if you are experiencing a difficult period. Remaining present in the NOW and keeping an eye out for the beautiful things in our lives, in the here and now, may at times be quite a challenge.

We are often inclined to look at things that still need to be done or what we do not have, instead of looking at everything that is already there. Dwelling on what is good in your life instantly causes a shift in your mindset and your emotions. Perhaps you know the power of consciously dwelling on the things that you are grateful for. Just try to write down three things that you are thankful for every day, for a month. From a small gesture to a great achievement. You will automatically feel happier.

In the book 'The Happiness Project' by Gretchen Rubin, she beautifully describes how gratitude and happiness are interrelated:

"Thankfulness is essential for happiness. Research shows that people who are constantly thankful, are happier and more satisfied with their lives. They feel physically healthier and do more exercise. Thankfulness ensures that you are not jealous because you are happy with what you have; you are not consumed by the desire to want something different or to want even more. This makes it easier to get around with the resources you have and to be generous to others. Thankfulness grows tolerance, you are less likely to be disappointed in someone if you feel grateful towards him or her. Gratitude brings you also in touch with the world of nature because one of the easiest things to be thankful for is the beauty of nature."

Wise and successful people do not let themselves be limited by disappointment or bitterness. In other words, they appreciate and enjoy life. You can easily recognise wise and successful people because they are always in a state of thankfulness. They are thankful for their lives, their successes, their opportunities, and their setbacks. They see their setbacks as lessons that teach them how to do things better and how to improve upon themselves

If you have set a specific goal and you have the feeling that it is going to take a while before you reach it, then look back and be thankful for the progress that you have already made. Congratulate yourself on all the accomplishments and realise that it is only a matter of time before you reach your goal. Write down your milestones to get a better view of what you have already achieved. By appreciating the steps you have already taken, you confirm that you are on your way to success.

If you notice that you have a lot on your mind (because there are too many bills or people are putting too many demands on you), try to appreciate the greater and more important things in your life. Start by being thankful for being alive. Appreciate the food that you eat, the roof over your head, the fresh air that you breathe and the clean water you drink. By cherishing these things, you can move from a state of worry to a state of ease and of bliss.

By being thankful, you focus your intention and attention to the things that you find pleasant rather than the things that you do not wish in your life. This allows you to attract the positive things in life, thereby bringing you more abundance.

# Chapter 18: Trust and Let Go!

In the book 'Ordering from the Cosmic Kitchen' by Patricia Crane, the art of manifesting is explained by comparing it to eating out. You choose a restaurant based on what you would like to eat at that moment. You decide carefully from the menu and then you place your order. Then you trust that the cook is doing his utmost to prepare a delicious meal for you and that it will be served within a reasonable time.

You do not constantly walk into the kitchen to see if they are really working on your order, or to see how your meal is being prepared.

The laws of the universe work in exactly the same way. You order what makes you really happy and what you feel like. Then you let it go, trusting that your order will be delivered at exactly the right time. This is obviously the difficult part because this is where you will be faced with your fears, limiting convictions and your resistances.

Trust gives you a carefree feeling. You let everything wash over you, you do not worry, and you assume that good things will happen to you. You can have confidence in people; you basically assume that people will have your best interest at heart. You can trust on what you are doing, in your own abilities; you will, for example, assume that you will make your exam well. You can also have faith in a religion or in life in general; you will not worry about your future, and you know that you will fare well.

The key is to not worry about the question of HOW you are going to get there and to trust the universe, to trust yourself, and to trust life. And in parenting: To trust your children.

When a baby is born, and it is completely healthy, we do not doubt for a moment that this baby will learn to roll over, crawl and walk. We just assume that. We gradually lose trust in this child and sometimes in ourselves too, in our role as an educator. We often rear our children based on fear. We are afraid that our children:

- ✓ Will derail, get on the wrong path

- ✓ Will not fit into the system

- ✓ Will not be accepted if they are themselves

- ✓ Will take charge, and walk all over us

**With this book I invite you to:**

- ✓ Believe in your children; they are stronger and more flexible than we often give them credit for and they are really not out to get in trouble or work against us.

- ✓ Believe in yourself: You will reap what you sow. You might not see it right away, but all your lessons are stored somewhere.

- ✓ Believe in the relationship between you and your child and realise that you can invest herein, and that that is the basis.

# *Letting go of perfection*

A very important step to a happier life is letting go of perfection. Just as with every characteristic, there is not one that is all bad, or all good. Every characteristic will at some point become a pitfall in a certain context. Someone who is very cautious by nature and who likes to do things well, has, in basis a fine characteristic. The problem is that this can sometimes, in a certain context lead to a form of perfectionism, and perfectionism is a quality with positive and negative sides. Nearly everyone has a bit of perfectionism within him.

When perfectionism serves to hide a low self-worth in addition to an inclination to negative thinking, you can reach your pitfalls easier and quicker. You tilt the balance even quicker in your tendency of not wanting to or not being able to, make any mistakes, And it very well maybe that you will be perceived as fussy by others. Your environment and possibly even you may find your behaviour irritating.

When you tell yourself (often unconsciously) that you are not good enough, if the piece is not 100% in order, and you already suffer from low self-esteem as well as being your own worst critic, then you are stuck in a trap, and in a negative spiral because you believe that if you do not do something well, then you are not good, which is something you do not want. This is why you continuously keep doing your best to get it right.

The unpleasant part is that when the piece is finished, you only feel satisfied for just a fleeting moment (and sometimes not even that) because most of the time your inner critic is still able to find something that could have been done better. Or you tell yourself, from your low self-esteem, that what you have accomplished is not really a big deal. Nothing special at all.

Turn this negative spiral around! Try to realise that it is not about the end result or the end goal, but that it is about the process, about getting there. Enjoy the ride. See every step forward, no matter how small, as a step in the right direction.

Sometimes perfectionism is also procrastination. You will only do something when you have sorted everything in the minutest detail, you will only start out on your own when your business plan is perfect, and you will only go on a diet when the rest of your life is in order. Be honest, start before you are ready. Experience the power of doing.

Laugh at yourself from time to time. It really does not matter if it does not work out the first five times but rejoice at the victory when it all comes together the sixth time. This, in essence, is the charm of life.

## *Basic exercises to let go*

Take a deep breath while you are reading this and release all the tension in your body when you exhale. Relax your scalp, your forehead and face. Relax your tongue and your throat, loosen your shoulders. You can read this while relaxing completely. Do this now.

Breathe down deeply to your stomach and your pelvis. Relax your back. Continue breathing, while you loosen up your legs and feet in the end. Notice how much stress you are holding on to.

# Chapter 19: Manifestation is a Way of Life: Commitment, Passion, Enthusiasm

I have gathered all of my knowledge, expertise and life experiences in this book, to inspire you and help you along the way to take very concrete steps to make your dreams come true. I hope you realise that everything in life is possible. That anything you desire can be reached. But that it all begins with love for yourself, with the making of conscious choices, with believing in yourself, overcoming your fears and with the taking of inspired action.

As a family, we have set a seven-year plan, with our goals and our wishes. This plan helps everyone maintain their commitment when decisions have to be made, to stay focussed, and to keep experiencing the passion in everything we do. Start by visualising the final result. Where do you want to be in one year? In three years? In five? A lot of people do not have a vision of their lives, but without this vision, opportunities will pass you by without you even noticing them, and life will slip through your fingers. Setting goals from the heart is a powerful tool for manifestation, and with manifestation I mean, realising that which has thus far only existed in your mind.

Setting goals is often a rational and realistic process. We analyse what is feasible based on previous experiences or by an assessment that we make in our heads. We make a plan, and designate the exact steps that we have to take to execute the plan.

There is also a different way to reach your goal. And that is by stating your intent.

It is a similar process to setting your goal, but the difference is that you do not worry about HOW to get there. You actually just indicate the result (your goal) that you want, and you relinquish the control you have about the way you are going to achieve that result. That is a manifestation.

Never be stopped by your own limiting thoughts. Ask yourself every so often, what beliefs you have that are not true. Liberate yourself from all of these so-called truths that you have been carrying with you from a very early age, and create your own reality. This is your life, and you can shape it exactly as you want it. Live your own truth, walk your talk and practice what you preach. Herein true happiness lies. Being exactly who you want to be and therefore being.

Finally: Positive thinking, living and educating is a life attitude, a lifestyle. Dare to leave behind that which limits you. Say 'yes' to yourself, to your truth. By doing this, you will open yourself up to receive the abundant stream of the universe, which only wishes to give you the best. It is an inner change that will change everything externally.

Have faith in the flow of life. Our family experiences many setbacks, but trust that these setbacks are all lessons and learning moments for us to be able to continue growing. Let go of the perfect image, of how everything should be and trust that everything will go exactly as it should go.

Your children will thank you, because by doing this, you become a more relaxed, satisfied and fun parent. And you also give your children the space and freedom to be themselves and to chase their own dreams with confidence.

## Important lessons and insights from Part 6

### For yourself

- ✓ When you assume full responsibility for your life, everything is possible.

- ✓ You cannot always change the situation you are into, but you can change your attitude towards the things that hinder you.

- ✓ Your dreams and desires are the inspirations for the changes you want to bring to your life. Take them seriously!

- ✓ Forgiving others is a liberation of yourself.

- ✓ Life rewards action. Stay in action, the action is the answer to fears, doubts and insecurity.

- ✓ Do not let your limiting convictions hinder you. Ask yourself every day what you believe, and what is not true.

- ✓ Practice thankfulness, this lets you tune into the right frequency for more abundance and positivity.

- ✓ Trust yourself, your children, life and the universe. Things are the way they are and everything is exactly as it should be.

- ✓ Manifestation is a way of life.

### In relation to your child(ren)

- ✓ By living fully and limitlessly, you give your children the freedom to do the same.

Taking action, that is what Part 6 was about. Setting goals from the heart (and not just SMART) is an excellent first step on the road to your dream life. In my e-Book 'Setting goals from your heart', you will find a step by step plan, worksheets, a monthly- and a weekly planner to help shape to your life. From goals and intentions to bite-size bits and laid out in an achievable planning!

To gain access to this practical gift, go to: www.nolimitparenting.com/bonuses or scan this QR-code.

# *Acknowledgements*

This book would not have been possible without the support, inspiration and guidance of some very special people. Naturally, my gratitude goes out to my beautiful family. You are my inspiration for everything that I do, and you are my mirror.

I am so immensely proud of you and how we manage to always inspire each other in good and in difficult times, and how we manage to keep each other on the straight and narrow and always with mutual understanding. Thank you for the trust, space and the time you have given me to write this book. I love you!

A word of gratitude as well to Jolanda Pikkaart, who put me on the path of Marije van de Bovenkamp, when I was in search of an editor. It was a match made in heaven, there was an instant click and Marije edited my texts with lots of respect and precision. My manuscript became better for it, and it offered me a personal lesson immediately: Marije removed all 'buts' and 'haves' ;-).

Fiona Jones, developer of the online programme 'Author Express', has given me so many tips during the whole writing- and publishing process. Her keen eye and crystal clear ability assess kept me sharp and challenged me to deliver even more quality. I learnt a great deal from her about marketing, branding and design. Lessons that will serve me well in future!

Nadia Azarova who is responsible for the design of the cover as well as the design of the content and who patiently produced one version after the other. And who persevered and delivered a remarkable achievement in the end. Thank you very much, Nadia!

A lot of thanks also to all (ex) participants of my online programme, No Limit Parenting, who read the rough draughts and provided me with feedback and encouragement during this process: Danitza, Anne-Marije, Corine, Encarnita, Elise, Marjorie, Jennie, Ruth Abigail, Dianne, Glenda.

A thank you to everyone who read the manuscript and took time out of their busy schedules to write a review, before the book was even published: Ruth Abigail, Heleen, Madeleine, Marije.

A word of gratitude to all the mothers that I have been able to meet, during my career and offer guidance and support to and who have unknowingly, in no small part, helped encourage me to write this book.

And last but certainly not least, thank you to my fantastic (Facebook) community who have consistently offered feedback on concept covers, who have answered my questions along the way with great enthusiasm, and who have liked my posts every time, and who have also let me know that they have indeed benefited from my insights and my lessons. Thank you all very much for your involvement, your questions and remarks and your inspiration!

Thank you all very much!

# About the author

Monique Daal is a developmental psychologist, coach, trainer and as of 2002 is also an entrepreneur.

With over 20 years of experience in the support and guidance of parents with educational questions and the leading of various educational programmes, she discovered how important it is to live the life that you grant your children. Children mirror our own pain and lessons and provide us with a reason to work on ourselves. Happy parents pass this happiness on to their children. As adults, we can give our children tools to enable them to get the most out of their lives, to not be afraid to be themselves and to live up to their full potential in life.

Monique combines her knowledge and expertise as a psychologist with her own life experience and insights that she has gained through books, seminars and (online) courses in the fields of mindset, life skills, mindfulness and spirituality. In this way, she helps others to discover what it is that they really want in life and what it is that they actually wish to pass on to their children.

When that is clear, relaxation is achieved in work, in life and in education, and new perspectives are created. Her mission is to contribute to a new paradigm in the raising and education of children. And this means shifting the accent from all that, which has to happen (obligations) to all that, which can happen (possibilities). That we should prepare children a little less for that great job or a great career, and a bit more for a good and a happy life.

With her websites www.moniquedaal.com and www. nolimitparenting.com and her Facebook communities, Monique wants to inspire mothers all over the world to get the best out of themselves and to hand them the tools to achieve a happier and more fulfilling life.

Monique was born in The Netherlands, from an Indonesian mother and an Antillean father. She emigrated in 2009 to Curacao, in the Caribbean, with her husband and her four children. She has been living with her family in Sydney, Australia, since 2015.

Printed in the United States
By Bookmasters